REGENTS RENAISSANCE DRAMA SERIES

General Editor: Cyrus Hoy
Advisory Editor: G. E. Bentley

A KING AND NO KING

BEAUMONT AND FLETCHER

A King and No King

Edited by

ROBERT K. TURNER, JR.

UNIVERSITY OF NEBRASKA PRESS · LINCOLN

Publishers on the Plains
UNP

MANUFACTURED IN THE UNITED STATES OF AMERICA

Regents Renaissance Drama Series

The purpose of the Regents Renaissance Drama Series is to provide soundly edited texts, in modern spelling, of the more significant plays of the Elizabethan, Jacobean, and Caroline theater. Each text in the series is based on a fresh collation of all sixteenth- and seventeenth-century editions. The textual notes, which appear above the line at the bottom of each page, record all substantive departures from the edition used as the copy-text. Variant substantive readings among sixteenth- and seventeenth-century editions are listed there as well. In cases where two or more of the old editions present widely divergent readings, a list of substantive variants in editions through the seventeenth century is given in an appendix. Editions after 1700 are referred to in the textual notes only when an emendation originating in some one of them is received into the text. Variants of accidentals (spelling, punctuation, capitalization) are not recorded in the notes. Contracted forms of characters' names are silently expanded in speech prefixes and stage directions, and, in the case of speech prefixes, are regularized. Additions to the stage directions of the copy-text are enclosed in brackets. Stage directions such as "within" or "aside" are enclosed in parentheses when they occur in the copy-text.

Spelling has been modernized along consciously conservative lines. "Murther" has become "murder," and "burthen," "burden," but within the limits of a modernized text, and with the following exceptions, the linguistic quality of the original has been carefully preserved. The variety of contracted forms (*'em, 'am, 'm, 'um, 'hem*) used in the drama of the period for the pronoun *them* are here regularly given as *'em,* and the alternation between *a'th'* and *o'th* (for *on* or *of the*) is regularly produced as *o'th'*. The copy-text distinction between preterite endings in *-d* and *-ed* is preserved except where the elision of *e* occurs in the penultimate syllable; in such cases, the final syllable is contracted. Thus, where the old editions read "threat'ned," those of the present series read "threaten'd." Where, in the old editions, a contracted preterite in *-y'd* would yield *-i'd* in modern spelling (as in "try'd," "cry'd," "deny'd"), the word is here given in its full form (e.g., "tried," "cried," "denied").

Punctuation has been brought into accord with modern practices. The effort here has been to achieve a balance between the generally light pointing of the old editions, and a system of punctuation which, without overloading the text with exclamation marks, semicolons, and dashes, will make the often loosely flowing verse (and prose) of the original syntactically intelligible to the modern reader. Dashes are regularly used only to indicate interrupted speeches, or shifts of address within a single speech.

Explanatory notes, chiefly concerned with glossing obsolete words and phrases, are printed below the textual notes at the bottom of each page. References to stage directions in the notes follow the admirable system of the Revels editions, whereby stage directions are keyed, decimally, to the line of the text before or after which they occur. Thus, a note on 0.2 has reference to the second line of the stage direction at the beginning of the scene in question. A note on 115.1 has reference to the first line of the stage direction following line 115 of the text of the relevant scene.

CYRUS HOY

Vanderbilt University

Foreword

I must express my thanks to those who generously answered my pleas for help with various parts of this edition, particularly to Herbert Nash Dillard, Lomas L. Barrett, James A. Brundage, Fredson Bowers, and Cyrus Hoy, the general editor of this series of texts. Part of the work was done in the Folger Shakespeare Library, whose excellent staff extended to me every courtesy. Some of the material in the Introduction appeared in an early form in *Renaissance Papers*; I am indebted to George Walton Williams, editor of that journal, for permission to use it here.

R. K. T.

Milwaukee
June, 1963

Contents

Abbreviations

Alden	R. M. Alden, ed. *A King and No King*. Boston, 1910.
Bond	R. W. Bond, ed. *"A King and No King,"* in *The Works of Francis Beaumont and John Fletcher*. Bullen's Variorum. 4 vols. London, 1904–1912.
Dyce	Alexander Dyce, ed. *The Works of Beaumont and Fletcher*. 11 vols. London, 1843–1846.
F	The eighth edition of *A King and No King*, the text included in the Second Folio collection of 1679.
Mason	John Monck Mason. *Comments on the Plays of Beaumont and Fletcher, with an Appendix, containing some further Observations on Shakespeare*. London, 1797.
OED	*Oxford English Dictionary*
om.	omitted
PMLA	*Publications of the Modern Language Association of America*
Q1	The first edition of *A King and No King*, a quarto of 1619
Q2	The second edition, a quarto of 1625
Q3	The third edition, a quarto of 1631
Q4	The fourth edition, a quarto of 1639
Q5	The fifth edition, a quarto of 1655
Q6	The sixth edition, a quarto of 1661
Q7	The seventh edition, a quarto of 1676
Q8	The ninth edition, a quarto of 1693
S.D.	stage direction
S.P.	speech prefix
Theobald	L. Theobald, T. Seward, and J. Sympson, eds. *The Works of Beaumont and Fletcher*. 10 vols. London, 1750.
Weber	Henry Weber, ed. *The Works of Beaumont and Fletcher*. 14 vols. Edinburgh, 1812.

Introduction

THE DRAMATISTS

"They lived together on the Banke side, not far from the Playhouse, both batchelors; lay together; had one Wench in the house between them, which they did so admire; the same cloathes and cloake, &c.; betweene them."[1] So John Aubrey reported the gossip about Francis Beaumont and John Fletcher, two young men of good family who began to write for the London stage in the early years of the seventeenth century. They apparently joined forces about 1607, when Beaumont would have been approximately twenty-three years old and Fletcher twenty-eight, and for five years or so their literary relationship seems to have been as close and as congenial as their living arrangements.[2] Each wrote at least one early play independently of the other, Beaumont *The Knight of the Burning Pestle* about 1607 and Fletcher *The Faithful Shepherdess* about 1608 or 1609, but they worked with each other (and on one play—*Beggar's Bush*—with Philip Massinger) to compose thirteen plays, including those which won for them rapid popularity and a permanent place in the history of the English drama: *Philaster* (1608–1610), *The Maid's Tragedy* (by 1611), and *A King and No King* (1611).[3] Their work was highly esteemed in

[1] *Aubrey's Brief Lives*, ed. Oliver Lawson Dick (1957), p. 21.

[2] The collaboration is usually thought to have begun in 1607, 1608, or 1609 (see, for example, E. K. Chambers, *The Elizabethan Stage* [1923], III, 216, and G. E. Bentley, *The Jacobean and Caroline Stage*, III [1956], 308), but Cyrus Hoy's finding that *The Woman Hater*, published in 1607, was a Beaumont original partially revised by Fletcher (see "The Shares of Fletcher and his Collaborators in the Beaumont and Fletcher Canon [III]," *Studies in Bibliography*, XI [1958], 85) suggests that the earliest of the three years may be the correct one. It was also in 1607 that the names of the playwrights were first publicly linked, they both having contributed commendatory verses to the first edition of Jonson's *Volpone*, which was published in that year.

[3] Hoy, "The Shares of Fletcher and His Collaborators in the Beaumont and Fletcher Canon (VII)," *Studies in Bibliography*, XV (1962), 85–86. The dates of composition are those assigned by Chambers, III, 222 ff.

their time. Thomas Fuller says of them that they "raised the English to equal the Athenian and Roman theatre,"[4] and John Webster in his preface to *The White Devil* (1612) singles them out for particular praise. Many other allusions to their plays make it clear that they were thought to be the rivals, and by some the superiors, of Shakespeare and Jonson.[5]

We do not know a great deal about the nature of the collaboration between them. Their contemporaries had the idea that Beaumont provided stability for Fletcher's volatile imagination. Aubrey learned from Bishop Earle that "Mr. Beaumont's maine Businesse was to lop the overflowings of Mr. Fletcher's luxuriant Fancy and flowing Wit";[6] Fuller adds that Beaumont brought "the ballast of judgment, and Fletcher the sail of phantasy; both compounding a poet to admiration."[7] The latest studies of the authorship of the so-called Beaumont and Fletcher canon (which actually includes the work of a number of other playwrights as well) shows that in those plays on which the two worked together certain of Fletcher's linguistic preferences, most notably *ye* and *'em,* do not appear in the profusion in which they are found elsewhere in Fletcher's work.[8] This fact may suggest that Beaumont was responsible for the final draft of these plays as well as for the composition of individual scenes; if this is so, he may very well have imposed on them their ultimate form. Certainly the lion's share of *A King and No King* appears to have been his; Professor Hoy attributes only IV.i–iii and V.i and iii to Fletcher.[9] Fletcher, of course, may have had a considerable share in the shaping of the plot, as Herrick's commendatory verse in the Beaumont and Fletcher First Folio would have us believe;[10] but commendatory verse generally seems to have been more pious than accurate.

The collaboration probably ended about 1613 when Beaumont married an heiress, Ursula Isley, and moved to the country. He

---

[4] *The Worthies of England,* ed. John Freeman (1952), p. 439.

[5] See the survey of Beaumont and Fletcher's contemporary reputation in Lawrence B. Wallis, *Fletcher, Beaumont, and Company* (1947), chap. 1.

[6] *Brief Lives,* p. 21.

[7] *Worthies,* p. 439.

[8] See Hoy, *Studies in Bibliography,* XI (1958), 85 ff.

[9] *Ibid.,* p. 91.

[10] See Wallis, pp. 195–196.

died in 1616. John Fletcher lived on in London and may be the man of that name who married a Joan Herring at St. Saviour's, Southwark, in 1612. It is pleasant to think, as Professor Chambers has suggested,[11] that it is to him Oldwit refers in Shadwell's *Bury Fair*:

> I knew Fletcher, my friend Fletcher, and his maid Joan. Well, I shall never forget him. I have supped with him at his house on the Bankside: he loved a fat loin of pork of all things in the world. And Joan his maid had her beer-glass of sack, and we all kissed her, i'faith, and were as merry as passed.
>
> (I.i)

He continued to turn out a great many plays, sometimes working alone but more often with one or more collaborators, a list of whom includes nearly everyone of consequence who wrote for the Jacobean theater—Massinger, Nathan Field, Thomas Middleton, William Rowley, John Ford, John Webster, George Chapman (perhaps, in *Rollo, Duke of Normandy*), and Shakespeare (probably in *The Two Noble Kinsmen* and possibly in *Henry VIII* and the lost *Cardenio*).[12] He died, Aubrey says of the plague, in 1625.

SOURCES

Fletcher's most fortunate collaboration, however, was with Beaumont, and *A King and No King* was written when both men were near the peak of their literary powers. As far as is now known, the specific fiction on which the drama is based was the invention of the playwrights, although some of the ideas it contains were common enough in the literature of the Renaissance. The basic theme of the main plot, that of incest averted by a happy discovery of true identity, is widely found. It is hinted at in the anonymous Spanish tale of the Abencerraje and the beautiful Jarifa, which made its way into Italian in the *Dugento Novelle del signore Celio Malespini* (II.xxxvi) and into English in Yong's translation of Montemayor's *Diana* (I.iv). The theme is more

[11] *The Elizabethan Stage,* III, 314.
[12] See Hoy, "Fletcher (VII)," *Studies in Bibliography,* XV (1962), 85–86.

explicitly treated in Juan de Timoneda's *Patrañuelo* (I.i) and the related play of Alonso de la Vega, *Tolomea*. In addition to the matter of the supposed brother and sister who fall in love, Timoneda's tale is further linked with *A King and No King* in that part of its action takes place in Armenia. The incest theme is also present in Fauchet's story of Thierry of France in *Lez Antiquitez et Histoires Gauloises et Françoises*, the source, it is thought, of Beaumont and Fletcher's *Thierry and Theodoret*.[13] Another parallel is found in *Il Novellino* of Masuccio of Salerno (III.xlii), a story which does not deal with incest but which does tell of a queen of Poland who accepts as her own the son of another woman under terms much the same as those promised by Arane to Gobrius when he gave her the infant Arbaces.[14] Moreover, the authors drew the names of some of their characters and a few plot details directly or indirectly from the ancient historians. In the *Bibliotheca historica* (II.xxiv ff.), Diodorus Siculus describes the downfall of Sardanapalus at the hands of a Median prince named Arbaces. Xenophon in the *Cyropædia* tells of Cyrus' friendship for Tigranes, a young Armenian prince (III.i *et passim*); of the acceptance by Cyrus of the service of Gobryas, an aged Assyrian, whose strong love for his son and whose wish (frustrated in the *Cyropædia*) to marry his daughter to the Assyrian prince (IV.vi) recall both Gobrius and Ligones in *A King and No King*; and of Araspes, a young Median, who falls so violently in love with Panthea, "the most beautiful woman of all Asia," that he threatens to ravish her when she refuses his advances (VI.i). In Plutarch's *Lucullus* there is a Tigranes, pompous and passionate ruler of Armenia, who, in something like Arbaces' manner, styles himself King of Kings. On one occasion this Tigranes asks an ambassador from Mithridates, who wants Tigranes to aid him against the Romans, what his own advice would be. Metrodorus,

---

[13] See A. H. Thorndike, *The Influence of Beaumont and Fletcher on Shakespeare* (1911), pp. 80–82.

[14] Of the two dramatists, Fletcher at least seems to have known Spanish: see T. P. Harrison, "A Probable Source of Beaumont and Fletcher's *Philaster*," *PMLA*, XLI (1926), 294, and E. M. Wilson, "Did Fletcher Read Spanish?" *Philological Quarterly*, XXVII (1948), 187–190. The conclusions of V. M. Jeffery, "Italian Influences on Fletcher's *Faithful Shepherdess*," *Modern Language Review*, XXI (1926), 147–158, imply that he may also have had some Italian.

Mithridates' emissary, replies "that as an ambassador he urged consent, but as an adviser he forbade it,"[15] words rather like those spoken in the play by Ligones to Tigranes on the subject of the prince's marriage to Spaconia (V.ii.63–67). Herodotus also speaks of the daughter of Gobryas as the first wife of Darius, and of a Mardonius, a Persian military commander and a close friend of Xerxes, as the son of Gobryas and the sister of Darius (VII.ii.5 *et passim*). Presumably the education of both the playwrights would have qualified them to consult the ancient writers in the original, but there is no indication that they relied specifically on any one of them.

Although *A King and No King* is based in part on classical materials, it obviously owes a debt also to the drama of its own time. The theme of incest averted had been treated comically in John Lyly's *Mother Bombie,* probably written about 1590. Bessus and the Swordmen are in the tradition of the *miles gloriosus,* and their inspiration may have been no farther from home than Pistol and Nym in *Henry V* or Captain Bobadill in *Every Man in His Humor.* Other similarities, none very strong, are described by D. M. McKeithan, *The Debt to Shakespeare in the Beaumont-and-Fletcher Plays* (1938), yet apparently unnoticed have been some striking parallels between *A King and No King* and *All's Well That Ends Well,* which seems to have been written less than ten years before it. Parolles, like Bessus, is a braggart warrior exposed, and, up to a point, Parolles is symbolically played off against Bertram just as Bessus is played off against Arbaces, a matter which is discussed below. It is even possible that Beaumont and Fletcher were influenced in their choice of a title by the series of paradoxes near the end of *All's Well,* V.iii—"he loved her, sir, and loved her not . . . he's guilty, and he is not guilty" and most precise of all ". . . thou art a knave, and no knave."

THE TRAGICOMEDY

A King and No King is in some respects typical of much of the Jacobean drama, the tone of which, it has often been said, is cynical, decadent, and spiritually empty. The relationship of Beaumont and Fletcher's tragicomedies to the spirit of their age is

[15] *Plutarch's Lives,* trans. Bernadotte Perrin (1928), II, 541.

variously described, perhaps most typically by Miss Ellis-Fermor, who sees them as offering a romantic escape from a reality of despondency and anxiety.[16] Miss Bradbrook believes that the slackening of the moral fiber apparent in these plays affected their literary quality. "The final test of these plays," she says, "is their language and here they are strikingly apart from the earlier drama. There is no verbal framework of any kind; the collapse of the poetic is to be directly related to the collapse of the moral structure, for they were interdependent."[17] Arthur Mizener, however, defends the playwrights against a specific charge of immorality by pointing out that they were, after all, no more immoral than anybody else:

> I cannot believe [he writes] that the attitude toward life implied by Beaumont and Fletcher's plays is not a reflection of the attitude which dominated the society for which they wrote and of which they were a part, rather than the result of any special immorality in them. Unlike Webster and Jonson, they were not seriously in revolt against the values of a large part of their world. Their plays are complex and delicate projections of one of the attitudes widespread in their day, just as Dekker's plays are a confused and crude projection of another. The moral quality implicit in both is not primarily a personal but a group attitude. . . .[18]

Since Professor Mizener wrote, however, Alfred Harbage has made it clear that even as late as the first decade of the seventeenth century there were distinct differences in the moral atmosphere of plays written for the popular theaters (the Globe, the Fortune, and the Red Bull) and those written for the private or "coterie" theaters (the Whitefriars and the Blackfriars); the former generally exhibited and subscribed to the traditional moral and ethical values of Christian humanism, whereas the latter were "preoccupied with lust and murder or lust and money, and with the exhi-

[16] Una Ellis-Fermor, *The Jacobean Drama* (1953), pp. 2–4.

[17] M. C. Bradbrook, *Themes and Conventions of Elizabethan Tragedy* (1935), pp. 247–248.

[18] Arthur Mizener, "The High Design of *A King and No King*," *Modern Philology*, XXXVIII (1940), 137, n. 9.

bition of the foolish and the foul."[19] As Beaumont and Fletcher's early plays "seem all to have been prepared for the boy companies at the private theaters,"[20] it would not be surprising that their later collaborations reflect, at least to some extent, the values of the private stage, in spite of the fact that their original performances may have been at the Globe.[21] The modern consensus is that the dramatists had an unusually well developed feeling for theater; their tragicomedies are held to be very skillfully constructed to exploit all the emotional possibilities of their rather gaudy themes. Yet the opinion remains that these plays lack high seriousness of purpose and are morally shabby.

Some light can be cast not only on this judgment but also on the reasons for the contemporary popularity of the tragicomedies by examining *A King and No King* from the point of view of the audiences that first attended it, people who seem to have held in common certain basic beliefs and attitudes regardless of whether they patronized the public or the private theaters. During the preceding age, tragedy had shared little of its popularity with tragicomedy, although the "mongrel" form, to use Sidney's epithet, was being acted at least as early as the mid-sixteenth century.[22] One aspect of Elizabethan tragedy was its fundamental lack of sentimentality; it was founded on a tough code in which sin was invariably paid for with death. Human evil was explained in terms of a Christianized version of Peripatetic doctrine: sin resulted from a victory of Will over Reason, the conflict of these two psychological factors, which should have acted in harmony, being one of the most disastrous legacies of Adam's fall from grace. The nature of sin was in part determined by the degree of stimulation received by the Will from the passions: if the stimulation was great enough to cause Will to override a reluctant Reason, venial sin resulted, but if the stimulation was so great that Reason itself became

[19] *Shakespeare and the Rival Traditions* (1951), p. 71 *et passim*.
[20] Bentley, III, 308.
[21] The title pages of *A King and No King* Q1 (see below, p. xxvi) and *Philaster* Q1 (1620) and Q2 (1622) say that they were acted at the Globe, but subsequent editions of both plays announce performance at the Blackfriars.
[22] See Marvin T. Herrick, *Tragicomedy* (1955), pp. 224 ff.

perverted and enslaved by Will, mortal sin resulted.[23] Thus, as Professor Lily Campbell has explained, tragic heroes were distinguished from villains by the extent to which Reason played a part in the commission of their sins.[24] But the point to be emphasized here is that in Elizabethan tragedy, although salvation was open to the protagonist not tainted with mortal sin, there was no human happiness for him; the tragic view saw in the universe a system of unalterable justice which usually demanded the life of the protagonist as payment for his evil deeds.

In the tragic system of values, the unspeakable crime of incest led straight to mortal sin, yet it is just this crime which provides the focal point of *A King and No King*. Arbaces, brilliant young king of Iberia, and Beaumont and Fletcher's protagonist, has not seen his sister Panthea since her childhood, having been away many years at the wars. When he returns home victorious, her beauty strikes him such a blow that he falls irretrievably in love with her, and in spite of his awareness of her charm and beauty, which, as dictated by standard Renaissance Neoplatonism, are but the outward manifestations of her inward goodness, his love expresses itself as a fierce carnal appetite. Turning on this central situation, the play becomes a conflict, conventional in Elizabethan tragedy, between Reason and Will, stimulated in this case by the passion lust, and Beaumont and Fletcher attempt to enhance the dramatic value of the conflict by making their protagonist a man of unusual psychological complexity.

Arbaces is "vainglorious and humble, and angry and patient, and merry and dull, and joyful and sorrowful, in extremities, in an hour" (I.i.84–86). To emphasize his internal conflict further, the dramatists construct the play, as Professor Mizener has shown, in the manner of the old moralities, with Mardonius as the good and Bessus as the evil angel.[25] Mardonius is all that is reasonable and humane in Arbaces' personality; Bessus, who also has some of the comic characteristics of the Vice, is all that is unreasonable and bestial. Thus, Arbaces stands between Mardonius and Bessus very much as the protagonist of *The Castle of Perseverance* stands

[23] See Lily B. Campbell, *Shakespeare's Tragic Heroes* (1930), chaps. 6 and 10.
[24] *Ibid.*, p. 101.
[25] Mizener, p. 150.

between his good and evil angels or, to choose a much later example, very much as Prince Hal stands between the Lord Chief Justice and Falstaff.

These relationships are made quite clear. Mardonius, the bluff and outspoken old soldier, is Arbaces' mentor; it is he who can discern and preserve the virtue that is intermixed with Arbaces' folly. He is, therefore, necessary to Arbaces, and both he and the king know it (IV.ii.167–175). Although he loves him, Mardonius is well aware of Arbaces' weaknesses, and he will not demean himself by flattering what he cannot respect. He is never in doubt, as some temporarily are, about Bessus' true nature. Thus, Mardonius serves symbolically as a projection of Arbaces' Reason, a quality which, according to Arbaces, binds man's actions with curious rules, restricting and confining the Will. It is just this function that Mardonius performs with respect to Arbaces on the narrative level of the play.

Bessus operates on two levels, and his dual roles reinforce and inform one another. He is, of course, the comic relief; his buffoonery stands in contrast with the high emotionalism of the Arbaces theme. Furthermore, in a much debased way, he exhibits, and at the same time parodies, Arbaces' boastfulness.[26] But in his direct relationship with Arbaces, he is much more sinister. Unlike Mardonius he does not seek literally to control the king, but he does suggest foolishly (and amusingly) that he can be set on the same level with him. "By my troth, I wish'd myself with you," he says to Arbaces with regard to the combat in which Tigranes was vanquished (I.i.220), and, in replying to Panthea's question about the king's health, he states that Arbaces is as well "as the rest of us that fought are" (II.i.79). Nobody takes this seriously, of course, but apparently the dramatists want us to see Bessus as something more than just a humorous poltroon. His bestiality is several times hinted at: Bacurius calls him "Captain Stockfish" (V.iii.15), specifically because he is the object of much cudgeling, and when the king rages he slinks away like an animal (I.i.291). But his subhuman qualities are revealed most clearly in the excellent scene in which Arbaces seeks a bawd, first in Mardonius and then in him (III.iii). The passionate and heavy mood of the king's conversation with Mardonius is broken when Bessus enters making a

[26] *Ibid.*, p. 139.

ridiculous jest. "Away, you fool. The king is serious/ And cannot now admit your vanities," cries Mardonius. But Arbaces is quite ready to reject Reason and surrender to Will. He interjects, "No, let him stay, Mardonius, let him stay./ I have occasions with him very weighty,/ And I can spare you now." Mardonius once gone, the king can speak without the hedging that characterized his earlier approach to the question. Previously Arbaces had stated that "he that undertakes my cure must first/ O'erthrow divinity, all moral laws . . ." (III.i.196–197), and Bessus is not only willing but eager to serve him. However, Bessus' bland equanimity in the face of the terrible proposition so horrifies Arbaces that he recoils:

> But thou appearest to me after thy grant
> The ugliest, loathed, detestable thing
> That I have ever met with. Thou hast eyes
> Like flames of sulphur, which, methinks, do dart
> Infection on me, and thou hast a mouth
> Enough to take me in, where there do stand
> Four rows of iron teeth.
>
> .   .   .   .
>
> Hung 'round with curses, take thy fearful flight
> Into the deserts, where, 'mongst all the monsters,
> If thou find'st one so beastly as thyself,
> Thou shalt be held as innocent.
>
> (III.iii.161–167, 181–184)

Arbaces, driving Bessus out, resolves to control his passions, but Bessus takes no fearful flight. The king has only temporarily renounced the domination of his Will, and Bessus remains on the scene just as Arbaces' unlawful lust continues to burn.

Tigranes is also used symbolically to comment on Arbaces' plight; the parallel between the two is strongly enforced. Like Arbaces, Tigranes is a young and powerful king. He too falls in love with Panthea at first sight, and his passion is also illicit except that it is so in terms of a breach of faith with Spaconia rather than a breach of moral law. His return to rectitude in love occurs in one of the rapid shifts in character found often in Beaumont and Fletcher. His soliloquy at IV.ii.1–33 begins with recriminations against Spaconia for interfering with his hopes for Panthea and against himself for putting her in a position to do so.

But at line 11 his good sense seems to overtake him: he suddenly becomes conscious of his debt to his mistress and the contemptibleness of his inconstancy. His sin against the code of love he conceives as something "unmanly, beastly"; he has, like Arbaces but in a smaller way, suffered a lapse from human status,[27] and it is brought home forcibly to him that, king or no king, he must learn to control his passions if he expects to preserve his human decency. His suffering is less intense than Arbaces', but he, like his captor, pays for his doting and emerges with a considerably less inflated opinion of himself. "I know I have/ The passions of a man," he acknowledges (V.ii.87–88).

The relationship of Mardonius, Bessus, and Tigranes to Arbaces helps to emphasize the alteration which his character undergoes during the course of the action. He is a man who is being purged of pride,[28] and the imagery of the play suggests that the authors conceived of this purgation in terms of a descent of the chain of being. At the outset, Arbaces thinks of himself as a hero-king who is especially favored of the gods; as a king he stands in a relationship to his enemies and his subjects roughly equivalent to that in which a god stands with respect to mankind in general. His victorious arm is "propp'd by divinity" (I.i.128); his mission has been to "teach the neighbor world humility" (I.i.133), and his conquest of Tigranes has been "an act/ Fit for a god to do upon his foe" (I.i.139–140). In his orgy of self-glorification, he sets himself on a level with the gods by degrading his followers to the level of animals: when Mardonius reproaches him for boasting, he retorts:

> By heaven and earth,
> I were much better be a king of beasts
> Than such a people. If I had not patience
> Above a god, I should be call'd a tyrant
> Throughout the world. (I.i.232–236)

Those who cross him lose claim to humanity. When Mardonius continues to censure him, he says:

---

[27] Cf. Spaconia's comment: "The princess hates thee deadly and will sooner/ Be won to marry with a bull, and safer,/ Than such a beast as thou art" (IV.ii.67–69).

[28] Mizener, p. 138.

> Oh, that thy name
> Were great as mine; would I had paid my wealth
> It were as great, that I might combat thee.
> I would through all the regions habitable
> Search thee, and, having found thee, with my sword
> Drive thee about the world till I had met
> Some place that yet man's curiosity
> Hath miss'd of; there, there would I strike thee dead.
> Forgotten of mankind, such funeral rites
> As beasts would give thee thou shouldst have.
>
> (I.i.281–290)

But such language as this is characteristic of Arbaces only when he is in the grip of his passions; a shift in his mood results in a change in his concept of himself. He then becomes a man among men, concerned about the world's opinion (I.i.480–483). His sudden love for Panthea makes him especially aware of his manhood; he sees himself no longer as semi-divine but as palpably human—"for I am a man," he says, "and dare not quarrel with divinity" (III.i.130–131). In fact, the initial shock of his meeting with Panthea pushes him far down the chain of being. "Am I what I was?" he asks himself, and, as he stares at his kneeling sister through an extraordinary silence, Mardonius says:

> Have you no life at all? For manhood sake,
> Let her not kneel and talk neglected thus.
> A tree would find a tongue to answer her,
> Did she but give it such a lov'd respect.
>
> (III.i.101–104)

As Arbaces tries to regain his former dominant status, once again his language becomes that of the hero-king:

> She is no kin to me nor shall she be;
> If she were any, I create her none,
> And which of you can question this? My power
> Is like the sea, that is to be obey'd
> And not disputed with. (III.i.165–169)

To this absurdity the sycophantic Bessus answers for Arbaces' Will, "No, marry, is she not, an't please your majesty./ I never thought she was; she's nothing like you" (III.i.174–175). For the last time the king thinks of himself as superhuman: ". . . I stood stubborn and regardless by/ And, like a god incensed, gave no ear/ To all your prayers" (III.i.282–284). He soon realizes that sin has robbed him of any pretensions he might have had to godlike power (III.iii.88–92).

Mardonius knows that Arbaces' lust is a scourge justly laid upon him by heaven (III.iii.2–3). Indeed, the scourge is applied so heavily that Arbaces fears he has slipped through the level of humanity to the level of the beasts. Figuratively he becomes a bull, an animal whose destructive power and overt sexuality are especially appropriate to Arbaces' state. That part of himself which he has given over to lust he acknowledges as bestial; his resistance to lust, which deteriorates with increasing rapidity, is "all that's man" about him (IV.iv.21). Having abandoned his reason through rejection of Mardonius, he has lost "the only difference betwixt man and beast" (IV.iv.65). Why, then, he asks, should he not enjoy the freedom of the beast, since "whoever saw the bull/ Fearfully leave the heifer that he lik'd/ Because they had one dam?" (IV.iv.136–138).[29]

Throughout the play the power of the Will, corrupted by lust, is imaginatively equated with poison, infection, and disease. Thus, Panthea begs the overwrought Arbaces to speak to her, even though the speech be "poison'd with anger" that may strike her dead (III.i.100). To Arbaces, Panthea is a witch, a poisoner, for she has given him "poison in a kiss" (III.i.321); yet he recognizes that she is a perfect woman and is evil only because he makes her so. To her pathetic question, "Alas, sir, am I venom?" he replies:

> Yes, to me.
> Though of thyself I think thee to be in
> As equal a degree of heat or cold
> As nature can make, yet as unsound men
> Convert the sweetest and the nourishing'st meats
> Into diseases, so shall I, distemper'd,
> Do thee.   (IV.iv.26–32)

---

[29] Spaconia's prediction that the princess would rather marry a bull (i.e., Arbaces) than Tigranes has already been cited (above, note 27). In addition, Tigranes rather indirectly relates Arbaces and this particular beast by characterizing Arbaces' treatment of him as "subtler than the burning bull's/ Or that fam'd tyrant's bed" (III.i.269–270). This image also occurs in a similar context in *Philaster* (III.i.235).

An earlier occurrence of this idea brings the disease imagery into conjunction with the beast imagery:

> You are fair and wise
> And virtuous, I think, and he is blest
> That is so near you as your brother is;
> But you are naught to me but a disease,
> Continual torment without hope of ease.
> Such an ungodly sickness I have got,
> That he that undertakes my cure must first
> O'erthrow divinity, all moral laws,
> And leave mankind as unconfin'd as beasts,
> Allowing them to do all actions
> As freely as they drink when they desire.
>
> (III.i.190–200)

Arbaces' lust not only infects Panthea in stimulating a responding passion in her, but, like the plague, permeates the atmosphere in which all his followers move. Mardonius is particularly aware of its evil power (IV.ii.220–222). Under these circumstances, it is not surprising to find Bessus associated with the idea of sickness (III.iii.163–165). The imagery of disease, which is linked to the narrative level of the play through Arane's attempt to poison Arbaces, is especially apparent in the discovery scene. There Arbaces, whose passion will not let him hear Arane and Gobrius out, rails at the queen-mother:

> Adulterous witch,
> I know now why thou wouldst have poison'd me;
> I was thy lust which thou wouldst have forgot.
> Thou wicked mother of my sins and me,
> Show me the way to the inheritance
> I have by thee, which is a spacious world
> Of impious acts, that I may soon possess it.
> Plagues rot thee as thou liv'st, and such diseases
> As use to pay lust recompense thy deed.
>
> (V.iv.160–168)

To the discovery scene, the theme being developed and the imagery which is organic to it convey tragic implications. The imagery is drawn from the same subject matter, if not presented with the same depth of insight and poetic skill, as that which dominates, for instance, *Hamlet, King Lear,* and *The Duchess of Malfi;* it is used to link the narrative and the symbolic levels of the drama, to create and sustain the atmosphere in which the action takes place, and to lend a unity to the whole composition, increasing its emotional impact. On the level of theme, Beaumont and Fletcher show Arbaces' Reason so crumbling before his Will that at the beginning of the discovery scene he stands on the lip of mortal sin. He announces:

> It is resolv'd. I bore it whilst I could;
> I can no more. Hell, open all thy gates,
> And I will through them; if they be shut,
> I'll batter 'em, but I will find the place
> Where the most damn'd have dwelling. . . .
>
> (V.iv.1–5)

Later in the scene, however, the tragic mood is completely dispelled; Arbaces learns that he is not Panthea's brother, and thus his illicit lust is transformed, technically at least, into legitimate love. Not only that; even though the revelation of his true parentage makes him no king, his marriage to Panthea will restore him to the throne. With the incest problem side-stepped, it turns out that Will, not Reason, had been right all along, a point driven home by Bessus' fatuous, yet significant, remark: "Why, if you remember, fellow-subject Arbaces, I told you once she was not your sister; I said she look'd nothing like you" (V.iv.293–295).

Thematically the play becomes a kind of philosophical pipe-dream, in which Will has its way while Reason stands by and nods approvingly. Punishment for surrender to the passions vanishes, a subversion of the moral and intellectual code which had formed the basis for tragedy. It is probably for this reason that *A King and No King* has seemed to some readers immoral: indulgence becomes in it not only respectable but very nearly sanctified. And it is no wonder that *A King and No King* and plays like it gained a quick popularity. What member of a society which was characterized by a "falling off in the general discipline"[30] would not like to see his own licentious fantasies symbolically projected with such dramatic effectiveness? Not only was it titillating, but

[30] G. B. Harrison, "The National Background," *A Companion to Shakespeare Studies,* ed. Harley Granville-Barker and G. B. Harrison (1955), p. 183.

it must have been rather a relief to be told that there was a world where the standards of Christian humanism did not hold—where technicalities existed which permitted one to lie with one's sister or perhaps to gorge on such other exotic emotional confections as suited one's palate without having to pay with a moral illness that might last an eternity.

THE TEXT

A King and No King was published about eight years after it was written. The following entry was made in the Stationers' Register on August 7, 1618: "*M*ʳ *Blounte*. Entred for his Copie vnder the handes of Sʳ George Bucke and Mʳ Adames warden A play Called A King and noe Kinge." In the next year, the first edition, a quarto, appeared, bearing the following on its title page:

> [ornament]/ A King and no King./ Acted at the *Globe,* by
> his Maie-/ *sties Seruants.*// Written by *Francis Beamount,*
> and *Iohn Flecher.*// [woodcut]/ AT LONDON/ Printed
> for *Thomas Walkley,* and are to bee sold/ at his shoppe at
> the Eagle and Childe in/ *Brittans-Bursse.* 1619.

Between the date of entry in the Stationers' Register and the date of printing, the copy was evidently transferred from Edward Blount to Walkley, who was soon to be concerned in the publication of such other King's Men properties as *Philaster* (1620), *Thierry and Theodoret* (1621), and *Othello* (1622). The printer of Q1, unnamed in the imprint, was probably John Beale.[31]

Walkley's dedication of the book to Sir Henry Neville[32] allows us to make several inferences about the nature of the copy. The play, it is said, "formerly hath been received" by Walkley from Neville, who had given it his "approbation and patronage" and

---

[31] See W. W. Greg, *A Bibliography of the English Printed Drama to the Restoration,* II (1951), 505. Certain ornaments used in the book are known to have belonged to Beale. Greg suggests (*Shakespeare First Folio* [1955], p. 154, n. 1) that the entry of the copy to Blount may have been a blocking entry, that is, one made by a cooperative stationer at the theatrical company's instigation for the purpose of denying publication rights to another stationer. If he is right, Walkley would have had to come to terms with the King's Men and perhaps also with Blount in order to publish the play.

[32] See below, p. 2.

who, it is suggested, desired that it be printed. The indications are, then, that Walkley had obtained a text of the play directly from Neville. We should expect a text originally in the possession of a private person to be a scribal transcript of papers held by the acting company, and the uniformity of act headings, speech prefixes, and other details suggests that such a manuscript, written in a single hand, was probably the copy from which Q1 was set. As we shall see later, Neville's scribe apparently copied the authors' final draft of the play rather than the company's promptbook.

The second edition of the play appeared six years after the first. Its title page reads as follows:

A KING/ and/ NO KING./ Acted at the *Blacke-Fryars*, by his/ MAIESTIES Seruants./ *And now the second time Printed, according/ to the true Copie.//* Written by FRANCIS BEAMOVNT and/ IOHN FLECHER.// [ornament]// *LON-DON*,/ Printed for *Thomas Walkley*, and are to be sold at/ his shop at the Eagle and Childe in/ *Brittans-Burse*. 1625.

The Blackfriars, located in a more fashionable and more easily accessible part of London than the Globe, had become a second playhouse for the King's Men "late in 1609 or early in 1610,"[33] and by 1635 the company's chief economic interests were in it rather than in the older theater.[34] The announcement on the Q2 title page of performances of *A King and No King* in the new theater suggests that between 1619 and 1625 the company had recognized the play as a piece more to the taste of their sophisticated clientele than to that of their more conventional customers in the Bankside. The other change from the Q1 title page—the claim that Q2 was now printed "according to the true copy"—was a standard publisher's puff and has significance, as we shall see, only in a very limited and special way. The second edition was followed by seven more before the end of the seventeenth century, further testimony of the play's popularity, but textual interest is largely confined to the first two.

The Q2 version differs in several interesting ways from the Q1. The most important textual variations are the addition by Q2 of three lines in III.i, the correction of some Q1 errors of language, and the reassignment of a few speeches, but the most striking dif-

---

[33] Bentley, III, 308.
[34] Chambers, II, 425.

ferences are in the stage directions. Q2 supplies some lacking in Q1, and in many instances where both Q1 and Q2 give directions the Q2 version is fuller or more accurately placed. Moreover, the Q2 stage directions use phraseology which is technically theatrical, the kind of language usually associated with the company's promptbook. On these grounds it might with some reason be inferred that Q1 and Q2 were printed from different manuscripts, Q1 from a transcript of authorial fair copy and Q2 from prompt copy, but duplications of the Q1 line arrangement in Q2 prove that Q2 was printed from an annotated Q1. This apparent conflict in evidence was ingeniously resolved by Berta Sturman, who argued that the Q1 exemplum which served as Q2 copy had been used by the King's Men as their promptbook, the manuscript promptbook having been lost, possibly in the Globe fire of 1613.[35] This hypothesis seems essentially correct, but because of the Q2 addition in III.i, the authenticity of which there seems no reason to doubt, it is unlikely that the Q1 exemplum was prepared *in vacuo* for use as a promptbook but was rather compared with some authoritative manuscript—the foul papers, the fair copy, or, most likely, the manuscript promptbook itself, which may have been worn out or damaged rather than destroyed. The addition probably was made at the time the quarto was prepared for the prompter's use, and some of the changes from Q1 now found in Q2 may also have been made then. If the version of the play thus prepared was actually used as a promptbook, however, other alterations now found in Q2 may have been made later.

Bibliographical analysis shows that Q1 was composed seriatim, with the exception of Gathering A, which contains the title page, Walkley's dedication to Neville, and the first four pages of text. One workman set Gatherings B through G and another set Gatherings H through M (the last in the book) and A, probably in that order.[36] These matters are of some consequence in evaluating the degree of fidelity of the quarto text to the transcript from which it was set and in trying to determine what kind of manuscript underlay the transcript. Seriatim setting means that the compositors set the pages of each gathering in numerical order (page 2

[35] "The Second Quarto of *A King and No King*," *Studies in Bibliography*, IV (1951–1952), 166–170.

[36] See my "Printing of *A King and No King*, Q1," *Studies in Bibliography*, Vol. XVIII (1965).

after page 1, page 3 after page 2, and so on); therefore, they would not have had much reason to adjust the text to predetermined units of space by such means as altering lineation, omitting lines or words, or even adding material of their own manufacture as they might have done had they been setting by formes (in a quarto gathering, pages 2, 3, 6, and 7 and then pages 1, 4, 5, and 8, or vice versa, a method of composition often used in early printing houses). Thus, it is likely that the lineation of the quarto text corresponds closely to the lineation of the transcript. The extent to which the scribe adjusted lineation is, of course, unknown. Occasional passages throughout the play and at least two scenes (IV.iii and V.iii), both involving Bessus and the Swordmen, may have caused him trouble. The quarto lines the first of these scenes largely as verse, the second largely as prose. Actually both contain verse, sometimes quite irregular, interspersed with some prose passages, this prosaic verse, it seems, being the vehicle which Fletcher, who wrote the Swordmen's scenes, chose to convey the heroic pretensions of Bessus and these comic characters. One suspects that in these instances the scribe, unable to scan them, made prose of some verse lines. The matter cannot be pressed very far, but there seems a good chance that the original manuscript was, in general, correctly lined. There are, as the textual notes to this edition show, errors both of omission and of commission in Q1, but no more than one would expect in a text transmitted through two agents, the scribe and the Q1 compositors. The stage directions of Q1 lack the strictly technical language of the theater, and in the stage direction introducing II.i there appears a ghost character, Mandane, who neither speaks nor is spoken to and who thus seems to be a vestige of an early stage of composition in which she was written a part. (One guesses that Mandane may once have been to Panthea about what Mardonius is to Arbaces, but that her role was suppressed in favor of Spaconia's.) These details suggest that the manuscript underlying the scribal copy was the authors' final draft, a document which contained a complete text correctly lined for the most part but also some loose ends of composition and perhaps some words that were of difficult legibility.

This leads to the question of the authenticity of passages or words in Q2 that differ from corresponding passages or words in Q1. Even if we assume that they were not alterations made by the company after the Q1 exemplum was annotated for use as a promptbook, it still seems that they would stand at three removes from the authors' papers, having passed first into the manuscript promptbook, then into the printed promptbook, and then into Q2. Q1 as a whole, however, probably stands at two removes from the authors' papers, having been transmitted through Neville's scribe and then through the Q1 compositors. In this edition, therefore, Q1 is followed in the main, and readings from Q2 are introduced into the text only when a good case can be made for corruption in Q1, even though in some instances Q2 provides readings that seem superior. This principle does not, however, preclude the adoption from Q2 of some apparently authentic readings, ranging in length from a word to several lines, that do not appear in Q1, probably because of eyeskip errors on the part either of the scribe or the compositors. As there is no information available about the proficiency of the compositors of the two quartos or of the scribe, it seems necessary to assume that the Q2 additions to the Q1 text are authentic unless they violate either sense or meter or seem themselves products of memorial error. The later editions furnish a guide for emendation in the few places where both Q1 and Q2 are defective, but they carry no independent authority.

For this edition all four copies of Q1 now located in the United States (one each in the Folger Shakespeare Library, the Henry E. Huntington Library, the Harvard University Library, and the Boston Public Library) were collated.[37] No press variants were observed. Substantive and semi-substantive departures from Q1 are recorded at the bottom of each page of the text. A historical collation of substantive variations between the present text and those of the editions of 1619 (Q1), 1625 (Q2), 1631 (Q3), 1639 (Q4), 1655 (Q5), 1661 (Q6), 1676 (Q7), 1679 (F), and 1693 (Q8) is given in Appendix A. Spellings are modernized throughout except in the textual notes and occasionally in the historical collation of early editions.

ROBERT K. TURNER, JR.

University of Wisconsin-Milwaukee

---

[37] The Boston Public copy is made up of Sheets A through D (less A1, A2) of Q1, the remainder being from Q3. Only the Q1 sheets have been collated.

A KING AND NO KING

To the Right Worshipful and Worthy Knight,
Sir Henry Nevill.

WORTHY SIR,

I present, or rather return, unto your view that which formerly hath been received from you, hereby effecting 5
what you did desire. To commend the work in my un-learned method were rather to detract from it than to give it any luster. It sufficeth it hath your worship's ap-probation and patronage, to the commendation of the authors and encouragement of their further labors. 10
And thus wholly committing myself and it to your wor-ship's dispose, I rest ever ready to do you service not only in the like but in what I may.

THOMAS WALKLEY.

---

2. *Sir Henry Nevill*] Nevill(e) of Billingbear, Berkshire, was the son of Sir Henry Neville (1564?–1615), an Elizabethan courtier and diplo-mat, and father of Henry Neville (1620–1694), an active political figure and writer of lampoons. He was born in 1588, matriculated at Merton College, Oxford, in 1600, and proceeded B.A. in 1603. By 1614 he was a student at Lincoln's Inn, and he twice served as a Member of Parlia-ment (Joseph Foster, *Alumni Oxonienses* [1891], III [Early Series], 1058). Wood adds that he was also legier ambassador at Paris (*Athenae Oxonienses* [1661], I, 796). He died in 1629. C. M. Gayley suggests that the original owner of the manuscript to which Walkley apparently refers was the elder Sir Henry (*Francis Beaumont: Dramatist* [1914], pp. 145–149).

10. *their further labors*] This phrase, Dyce points out, is rather peculiar; it was presumably written in 1619, but Beaumont had died in 1616. Probably it argues no more than Walkley's lack of acquaint-ance with the playwrights, although Bond (p. 248) suggests that it alludes to the future publication of other Beaumont and Fletcher plays.

[The Names of the Actors

ARBACES, *King of Iberia*
TIGRANES, *King of Armenia*
GOBRIUS, *Lord Protector of Iberia and father of Arbaces*
BACURIUS, *an Iberian lord*   5
MARDONIUS ⎱
BESSUS   ⎰ *captains in the Iberian army*
LIGONES, *an Armenian statesman and father of Spaconia*
PHILIP, *servant of a Citizen's Wife*
TWO SWORDMEN   10
A BOY, *servant of Bessus*
ARANE, *the Iberian Queen Mother*
PANTHEA, *her daughter*
SPACONIA, *an Armenian lady, daughter of Ligones*
TWO CITIZENS' WIVES   15
GENTLEMEN, ATTENDANTS, SERVANTS, MESSENGERS, CITIZENS,
    AND WAITING-WOMEN

Scene

In the first act, Armenia;
afterwards, the Iberian court]   20

---

1. *The Names of the Actors*] A dramatis personae was first included
by Q3. Q7 gives the cast of the play "as it is now acted at the Theatre
Royal by His Majestie's Servants" (1676).
   4. *Gobrius*] The name is spelled *Gobrias* in Q1 from its first use at
I.i.447 (C1) to the stage direction beginning III.i (E1ᵛ), a total of five
occurrences. At the latter point Compositor A began to spell *Gobrius*,
and this form was used some twenty times throughout the rest of the
play except for one reversion to *Gobrias* at IV.i.1 (G3ᵛ), which is still
within Compositor A's stint. It is not clear why the name is spelled in
the two ways, but as the *-us* form appears in the work of both compositors, it would seem to be the more authoritative.

A King and No King

Enter Mardonius *and* Bessus.

MARDONIUS.

Bessus, the king has made a fair hand on't; h'as ended
the wars at a blow. Would my sword had a close basket
hilt to hold wine and the blade would make knives, for
we shall have nothing but eating and drinking.

BESSUS.

We that are commanders shall do well enough.   5

MARDONIUS.

Faith, Bessus, such commanders as thou may; I had as
lieve set thee *perdu* for a pudding i'th' dark as Alexander
the Great.

BESSUS.

I love these jests exceedingly.

MARDONIUS.

I think thou lov'st them better than quarreling, Bessus;   10
I'll say so much i'thy behalf. And yet thou art valiant
enough upon a retreat; I think thou wouldst kill any
man that stopped thee, an thou couldst.

BESSUS.

But was not this a brave combat, Mardonius?

MARDONIUS.

Why, didst thou see't?   15

BESSUS.

You stood with me.

---

1. *made . . . on't*] made a great success of it. The phrase was often
used ironically (*OED, sb.* 45.a).

7-8. *set . . . Great*] "set thee perdu" means "put you in an exposed
and dangerous post" (*OED, adj.* A.3.a). Mardonius says, "I had just
as soon put you in a crucial position as I would Alexander the Great, as
long as the enemy is only a pudding."

14. *brave*] excellent, worthy.

MARDONIUS.

I did so, but methought thou wink'st every blow they strake.

BESSUS.

Well, I believe there are better soldiers than I that never saw two princes fight in lists. 20

MARDONIUS.

By my troth, I think so too, Bessus—many a thousand; but certainly all that are worse than thou have seen as much.

BESSUS.

'Twas bravely done of our king.

MARDONIUS.

Yes, if he had not ended the wars. I am glad thou dar'st 25 talk of such dangerous businesses.

BESSUS.

To take a prince prisoner in the heart of his own country in single combat!

MARDONIUS.

See how thy blood cruddles at this. I think thou wouldst be contented to be beaten in this passion. 30

BESSUS.

Shall I tell you truly?

MARDONIUS.

Ay.

BESSUS.

I could willingly venter for it.

MARDONIUS.

Um, no venter neither, good Bessus.

BESSUS.

Let me not live if I do not think it is a braver piece of 35 service than that I'm so fam'd for.

---

18. *strake*] i.e., struck.

20. *in lists*] man-to-man. Lists are "the palisades . . . enclosing a space set aside for tilting" (*OED, sb.*³ 9).

24. *bravely*] worthily.

29. *cruddles*] i.e., curdles.

33, 34. *venter*] i.e., venture.

MARDONIUS.

Why, art thou fam'd for any valor?

BESSUS.

I fam'd? Ay, I warrant you.

MARDONIUS.

I am very heartily glad on't. I have been with thee ever
since thou cam'st o'th' wars, and this is the first word that   40
ever I heard on't. Prithee, who fames thee?

BESSUS.

The Christian world.

MARDONIUS.

'Tis heathenishly done of them; in my conscience thou
deserv'st it not.

BESSUS.

Yes, I ha' done good service.   45

MARDONIUS.

I do not know how thou may'st wait of a man in's chamber or thy agility in shifting a trencher, but otherwise no
service, good Bessus.

BESSUS.

You saw me do the service yourself.

MARDONIUS.

Not so hasty, sweet Bessus. Where was it? Is the place   50
vanish'd?

BESSUS.

At Bessus' Desperate Redemption.

MARDONIUS.

Bessus' Desperate Redemption! Where's that?

BESSUS.

There where I redeem'd the day; the place bears my
name.   55

MARDONIUS.

Prithee, who christen'd it?

BESSUS.

The soldier.

37. Why, art] *Q2*; Why art *Q1*.

_____

46. *of*] on.
47. *trencher*] wooden platter.
57. *The soldier*] the troops.

MARDONIUS.

If I were not a very merrily dispos'd man, what would
become of thee? One that had but a grain of choler in
the whole composition of his body would send thee of an   60
errand to the worms for putting thy name upon that
field. Did not I beat thee there i'th' head o'th' troops
with a truncheon because thou wouldst needs run away
with thy company when we should charge the enemy?

BESSUS.

True, but I did not run.   65

MARDONIUS.

Right, Bessus; I beat thee out on't.

BESSUS.

But came not I up when the day was gone and redeem'd
all?

MARDONIUS.

Thou know'st, and so do I, thou meant'st to fly, and, thy
fear making thee mistake, thou ran'st upon the enemy;   70
and a hot charge thou gav'st, as, I'll do thee right, thou
art furious in running away, and I think we owe thy fear
for our victory. If I were the king, and were sure thou
wouldst mistake always, and run away upon the enemy,
thou shouldst be general, by this light.   75

BESSUS.

You'll never leave this till I fall foul.

MARDONIUS.

No more such words, dear Bessus. For though I have ever
known thee a coward and therefore durst never strike
thee, yet if thou proceed'st, I will allow thee valiant and
beat thee.   80

---

58. merrily] *Q2*; meerely *Q1*.   69. meant'st] *Q2*; mean'st *Q1*.

---

59. *but . . . choler*] the least bit inclined to anger. Choler was one
of the four humors, body fluids which arose from the four elements of
which all created matter, including the human body, was composed.
One whose mind was influenced by the choler in his body tended to be
irascible.

60. *of an*] on an.

62. *head*] front.

66. *on't*] of it.

76. *fall foul*] quarrel.

BESSUS.

Come, come—our king's a brave fellow.

MARDONIUS.

He is so, Bessus; I wonder how thou com'st to know it.
But if thou wert a man of understanding, I would tell
thee he is vainglorious and humble, and angry and patient, and merry and dull, and joyful and sorrowful, in   85
extremities, in an hour. Do not think me thy friend for
this, for if I car'd who knew it, thou shouldst not hear it,
Bessus. Here he is, with the prey in his foot.

Enter Arbaces *and* Tigranes, *with two* Gentlemen *and attendants.*

ARBACES.

Thy sadness, brave Tigranes, takes away
From my full victory; am I become   90
Of so small fame that any man should grieve
When I o'ercome him? They that plac'd me here
Intended it an honor large enough
For the most valiant living but to dare
Oppose me single, though he lost the day.   95
What should afflict you? You are free as I.
To be my prisoner is to be more free
Than you were formerly, and never think
The man I held worthy to combat me
Shall be us'd servilely. Thy ransom is   100
To take my only sister to thy wife—
A heavy one, Tigranes, for she is
A lady that the neighbor princes send
Blanks to fetch home. I have been too unkind
To her, Tigranes. She but nine year old,   105
I left her, and ne'er saw her since; your wars

88.1. *Enter . . . attendants.*] *Enter
Arbaces and Tigranes, with attendants. Q1; Enter &c. Senet
Flourish./ Enter* Arbaces *and* Tigranes *two Kings, &c./ The two
Gentlemen. Q2, 7–8; . . . Kings
and two Gentlemen. Q3–6, F.*
90. full] *Q2;* fall *Q1.*

---

88. *prey in his foot*] i.e., like a falcon.
104. *Blanks*] treaties, marriage bonds, or similar documents with the
conditions left blank so that Arbaces might fill in whatever terms he
chooses.

Have held me long and taught me, though a youth,
The way to victory. She was a pretty child
Then; I was little better. But now fame
Cries loudly on her, and my messengers   110
Make me believe she is a miracle.
She'll make you shrink, as I did, with a stroke
But of her eye, Tigranes.

TIGRANES.   Is it the course of
Iberia to use their prisoners thus?
Had Fortune thrown my name above Arbaces',   115
I should not thus have talk'd, for in Armenia
We hold it base. You should have kept your temper
Till you saw home again, where 'tis the fashion
Perhaps to brag.

ARBACES.   Be you my witness, Earth,
Need I to brag? Doth not this captive prince   120
Speak me sufficiently, and all the acts
That I have wrought upon his suffering land?
Should I then boast? Where lies that foot of ground
Within his whole realm that I have not past
Fighting and conquering? Far then from me   125
Be ostentation. I could tell the world
How I have laid his kingdom desolate
With this sole arm propp'd by divinity,
Stripp'd him out of his glories, and have sent
The pride of all his youth to people graves,   130
And made his virgins languish for their loves,
If I would brag. Should I, that have the power
To teach the neighbor world humility,

113. S.P. TIGRANES.] Q2; om. Q1.

---

113. S.P. TIGRANES.] The omission of this speech prefix leads Miss
Berta Sturman to think that l. 113 was written as one line in the
manuscript from which Q1 was printed, the word *Tigranes* being intended there as the speech prefix and not the last word of Arbaces'
speech (see *Studies in Bibliography*, IV [1951–1952], 167–168). If she is
right, *Tigranes* should be omitted from the text, but to do so would be
to make the line even less regular than it presently is. It seems more
likely that the name stood in the manuscript as part of the text and
that the speech prefix was omitted through eyeskip.
121. *Speak me*] testify.

  Mix with vainglory?

MARDONIUS [*Aside*]. Indeed, this is none?

ARBACES.

  Tigranes, no; did I but take delight   135
  To stretch my deeds, as others do, on words,
  I could amaze my hearers.

MARDONIUS [*Aside*].   So you do.

ARBACES.

  But he shall wrong his, and my, modesty
  That thinks me apt to boast. After an act
  Fit for a god to do upon his foe,   140
  A little glory in a soldier's mouth
  Is well becoming; be it far from vain.

MARDONIUS [*Aside*].

  It's pity that valor should be thus drunk.

ARBACES.

  I offer you my sister, and you answer
  I do insult, a lady that no suit   145
  Nor treasure nor thy crown could purchase thee,
  But that thou fought'st with me.

TIGRANES.   Though this be worse
  Than that you spoke before, it strikes not me;
  But that you think to overgrace me with
  The marriage of your sister troubles me;   150
  I would give worlds for ransoms, were they mine,
  Rather than have her.

ARBACES.   See if I insult
  That am the conqueror and for a ransom
  Offer rich treasure to the conquered
  Which he refuses, and I bear his scorn!   155
  It cannot be self-flattery to say,
  The daughters of your country set by her
  Would see their shame, run home, and blush to death
  At their own foulness. Yet she is not fair
  Nor beautiful; those words express her not. 160
  They say her looks are something excellent
  That wants a name. Yet were she odious,

162. name. Yet] *Q2*; name yet: *Q1*.

148. *strikes*] impresses.

Her birth deserves the empire of the world,
Sister to such a brother, that hath ta'en
Victory prisoner and throughout the earth   165
Carries her bound, and should he let her loose,
She durst not leave him. Nature did her wrong
To print continual conquest on her cheeks
And make no man worthy for her to take
But me that am too near her, and as strangely   170
She did for me. But you will think I brag.
MARDONIUS [*Aside*].
    I do, I'll be sworn. Thy valor and thy passions sever'd
would have made two excellent fellows in their kinds. I
know not whether I should be sorry thou art so valiant
or so passionate. Would one of 'em were away.   175
TIGRANES.
    Do I refuse her that I doubt her worth?
Were she as virtuous as she would be thought,
So perfect that no one of her own sex
Would find a want, had she so tempting fair
That she could wish it off for damning souls,   180
I would pay any ransom twenty times
Rather than meet her married in my bed.
Perhaps I have a love where I have fix'd
Mine eyes, not to be mov'd, and she on me.
I am not fickle.
ARBACES.   Is that all the cause?   185
    Think you, you can so knit yourself in love
To any other that her searching sight
Cannot dissolve it? So, before you tried,
You thought yourself a match for me in fight.
Trust me, Tigranes, she can do as much   190
In peace as I in war; she'll conquer too.
You shall see, if you have the power to stand

---

178. one] *Q2*; owne *Q1*.   180. for] *Q2*; her *Q1*.

171. *She*] i.e., Nature.
173. *in their kinds*] in their own natural ways.
176. *that*] because.
179. *so tempting fair*] such a tempting beauty.
180. *for damning souls*] lest it damn souls.

> The force of her swift looks. If you dislike,
> I'll send you home with love and name your ransom
> Some other way, but if she be your choice,   195
> She frees you. To Iberia you must.

TIGRANES.

> Sir, I have learnt a prisoner's sufferance
> And will obey, but give me leave to talk
> In private with some friends before I go.

ARBACES.

> Some two await him forth and see him safe,   200
> But let him freely send for whom he please,
> And none dare to disturb his conference.
> I will not have him know what bondage is
> Till he be free from me.
>
>   *Exeunt* Tigranes [*and two attendants*].
>   This prince, Mardonius,
> Is full of wisdom, valor, all the graces   205
> Man can receive.

MARDONIUS.   And yet you conquered him?

ARBACES.

> And yet I conquered him, and could have done
> Hadst thou join'd with him, though thy name in arms
> Be great. Must all men that are virtuous
> Think suddenly to match themselves with me?   210
> I conquered him and bravely, did I not?

BESSUS.

> And please your majesty, I was afraid at first—

MARDONIUS.

> When wert thou other?

ARBACES.

> Of what?

BESSUS.

> —That you would not have spied your best advantages, 215
> for your majesty, in my opinion, lay too high methinks;

196. Iberia] *Q2; Ileria Q1.*   *Q1 (after l. 203); Exit Tigranes.*
204. S.D. *Exeunt* Tigranes.] *Exe.*   *Q2–8, F (after l. 203).*

---

200. *await*] attend.
216. *lay too high*] used too high a fighting posture.

under favor, you should have lain thus.

MARDONIUS.

Like a tailor at a wake.

BESSUS.

And then, if't please your majesty to remember, at one
time—by my troth, I wish'd myself with you.   220

MARDONIUS.

By my troth, thou wouldst have stunk 'em both out o'th'
lists.

ARBACES.

What to do?

BESSUS.

To put your majesty in mind of an occasion: you lay
thus, and Tigranes falsified a blow at your leg, which you   225
by doing thus avoided; but if you had whipp'd up your
leg thus and reach'd him on th'ear, you had made the
blood-royal run about's head.

MARDONIUS.

What country fence-school didst thou learn that at?

ARBACES.

Puft! Did I not take him nobly?

MARDONIUS.   Why, you did,   230
And you have talk'd enough on't.

ARBACES.   Talk'd enough!
While you confine my words?—By heaven and earth,
I were much better be a king of beasts
Than such a people. If I had not patience
Above a god, I should be call'd a tyrant   235
Throughout the world. They will offend to death
Each minute.—Let me hear thee speak again
And thou art earth again. Why, this is like
Tigranes' speech, that needs would say I bragg'd.
Bessus, he said I bragg'd.   240

221. stunk] *Q2*; sunke *Q1*.   231. Talk'd] *Q7*; Talke *Q1–6*.
228. -royal] *Q2*; om. *Q1*.

---

218. *wake*] festival (*OED, sb.*¹ 4.a and b and cf. IV.ii.220–221).
224. *occasion*] opportunity.
225. *falsified a blow*] feinted.

BESSUS.

    Ha, ha, ha.

ARBACES.   Why dost thou laugh?

    By all the world, I'm grown ridiculous

    To my own subjects. Tie me to a chair

    And jest at me! But I shall make a start

    And punish some, that other will take heed   245

    How they are haughty. Who will answer me?

    He said I boasted.—Speak, Mardonius;

    Did I?—He will not answer. Oh, my temper!

    I give you thanks above that taught my heart

    Patience; I can endure his silence.—What, will none   250

    Vouchsafe to give me audience? Am I grown

    To such a poor respect? Or do you mean

    To break my wind? Speak; speak soon, one of you,

    Or else, by heaven—

1 GENTLEMAN.   So please your—

ARBACES.   Monstrous!

    I cannot be heard out; they cut me off   255

    As if I were too saucy. I will live

    In woods and talk to trees; they will allow me

    To end what I begin. The meanest subject

    Can find a freedom to discharge his soul,

    And not I.—Now it is a time to speak;   260

    I harken.

1 GENTLEMAN.   May it please—

ARBACES.   I mean not you;

    Did not I stop you once? But I am grown

    To balk. But I desire, let another speak.

2 GENTLEMAN.

    I hope your majesty—

---

    253. *break my wind*] make me talk until I am short of breath.

    263. *To balk. But I desire*] Q2 and subsequent early editions read *To balke, but I defie*, which was changed by Theobald, on Seward's suggestion, to *To talk but idly*. Theobald speaks of this as a "beautiful Emendation," and it is, of the Q2 reading, but there is nothing wrong with the Q1 version if "to balk" is understood as "to be balked" or "a thing that is balked." Q2's *defie* looks like a simple misprint of Q1's *desire*.

ARBACES.   Thou drawest thy words
That I must wait an hour where other men   265
Can hear in instants. Throw your words away
Quick and to purpose; I have told you this.

BESSUS.
An't please your majesty—

ARBACES.
Wilt thou devour me? This is such a rudeness
As yet you never showed me, and I want   270
Power to command too, else Mardonius
Would speak at my request.—Were you my king,
I would have answered at your word, Mardonius.
I pray you speak, and truly; did I boast?

MARDONIUS.
Truth will offend you.

ARBACES.   You take all great care   275
What will offend me, when you dare to utter
Such things as these.

MARDONIUS.
You told Tigranes you had won his land
With that sole arm propp'd by divinity.
Was not that bragging and a wrong to us   280
That daily ventur'd lives?

ARBACES.   Oh, that thy name
Were great as mine; would I had paid my wealth
It were as great, that I might combat thee.
I would through all the regions habitable
Search thee, and, having found thee, with my sword   285
Drive thee about the world till I had met
Some place that yet man's curiosity
Hath miss'd of; there, there would I strike thee dead.
Forgotten of mankind, such funeral rites
As beasts would give thee thou shouldst have.

271. too] *Q2*; me *Q1*.

---

264. *drawest*] draw out, drawl.
265. *That*] so that.
271. *too*] Q1's *me* is probably a memorial error induced by *me* in
ll. 269 and 270.

BESSUS. The king 290
    Rages extremely; shall we slink away?
    He'll strike us.
2 GENTLEMAN.
    Content.
ARBACES.
    There I would make you know 'twas this sole arm.
    I grant you were my instruments and did 295
    As I commanded you, but 'twas this arm
    Mov'd you like wheels; it mov'd you as it pleas'd.—
    Whither slip you now? What, are you too good
    To wait on me?—Puff! I had need have temper,
    That rule such people; I have nothing left 300
    At my own choice. I would I might be private:
    Mean men enjoy themselves, but 'tis our curse
    To have a tumult that, out of their loves,
    Will wait on us whether we will or no.—
    Will you be gone?—Why, here they stand like death; 305
    My word moves nothing.
1 GENTLEMAN. Must we go?
BESSUS. I know not.
ARBACES.
    I pray you leave me, sirs.—I'm proud of this,
    That they will be entreated from my sight.
Exeunt all but Arbaces *and* Mardonius. [Mardonius *offers to go.*]
    Why, now they leave me all.—Mardonius!
MARDONIUS.
    Sir?
ARBACES. Will you leave me quite alone? Methinks 310
    Civility should teach you more than this,
    If I were but your friend. Stay here and wait.
MARDONIUS.
    Sir, shall I speak?
ARBACES. Why, you would now think much
    To be denied, but I can scarce entreat

299. Puff!] *Q2; om. Q1.*   308.1. *Exeunt* . . . Mardonius.] *Q2;*
306. S.P. 1 GENTLEMAN.] *Q2;* 2 *om. Q1.*
Gent. Q1.

301. *private*] (1) alone, (2) a private citizen.

What I would have. Do, speak.   315
MARDONIUS.

But will you hear me out?
ARBACES.

With me you article to talk thus. Well,
I will hear you out.
MARDONIUS.   Sir, that I have ever loved you   [*Kneels.*]
My sword hath spoken for me; that I do,
If it be doubted, I dare call an oath,   320
A great one, to my witness. And were you
Not my king, from amongst men I should
Have chose you out to love above the rest.
Nor can this challenge thanks. For my own sake
I should have doted, because I would have lov'd   325
The most deserving man, for so you are.
ARBACES.

Alas, Mardonius, rise; you shall not kneel.   [*Raises him.*]
We all are soldiers and all venter lives,
And where there is no difference in men's worths
Titles are jests. Who can outvalue thee?   330
Mardonius, thou hast lov'd me and hast wrong;
Thy love is not rewarded; but believe
It shall be better, more than friend in arms,
My father and my tutor, good Mardonius.
MARDONIUS.

Sir, you did promise you would hear me out.   335
ARBACES.

And so I will; speak freely, for from thee
Nothing can come but worthy things and true.
MARDONIUS.

Though you have all this worth, you hold some qualities
That do eclipse your virtues.
ARBACES.   Eclipse my virtues?
MARDONIUS.

Yes, your passions, which are so manifold that they ap- 340
pear even in this: when I commend you, you hug me for

---

317. *article*] make conditions.
324. *challenge*] claim.
328. *venter*] i.e., venture.

that truth; when I speak of your faults, you make a start
and fly the hearing. But—

ARBACES.

When you commend me! Oh, that I should live
To need such commendations. If my deeds   345
Blew not my praise themselves above the earth,
I were most wretched. Spare your idle praise.
If thou didst mean to flatter and shouldst utter
Words in my praise that thou thought'st impudence,
My deeds should make 'em modest. When you praise,   350
I hug you! 'Tis so false that wert thou worthy
Thou shouldst receive a death, a glorious death,
From me. But thou shalt understand thy lies;
For shouldst thou praise me into heaven and there
Leave me enthron'd, I would despise thee though   355
As much as now, which is as much as dust,
Because I see thy envy.

MARDONIUS.

However you will use me after, yet
For your own promise sake hear me the rest.

ARBACES.

I will, and after call unto the winds,   360
For they shall lend as large an ear as I
To what you utter. Speak.

MARDONIUS.   Would you but leave
These hasty tempers, which I do not say
Take from you all your worth, but darken 'em,
Then you would shine indeed.   365

ARBACES.

Well.

MARDONIUS.

Yet I would have you keep some passions, lest men should
take you for a god, your virtues are such.

ARBACES.

Why, now you flatter.

MARDONIUS.

I never understood the word. Were you no king and free   370
from these wild moods, should I choose a companion for
wit and pleasure, it should be you; or for honest to inter-

---

372. *for honest*] openly, without guile.

change my bosom with, it would be you; or wisdom to
give me counsel, I would pick out you; or valor to defend
my reputation, still I would find out you; for you are fit 375
to fight for all the world, if it could come in question.
Now I have spoke, consider to yourself, find out a use; if
so, then what shall fall to me is not material.

ARBACES.

Is not material? More than ten such lives
As mine, Mardonius. It was nobly said;   380
Thou hast spoke truth, and boldly—such a truth
As might offend another. I have been
Too passionate and idle; thou shalt see
A swift amendment. But I want those parts
You praise me for. I fight for all the world?   385
Give thee a sword, and thou wilt go as far
Beyond me as thou art beyond in years;
I know thou dar'st and wilt. It troubles me
That I should use so rough a phrase to thee;
Impute it to my folly, what thou wilt,   390
So thou wilt pardon me. That thou and I
Should differ thus!

MARDONIUS.   Why, 'tis no matter, sir.

ARBACES.

Faith, but 'tis; but thou dost ever take
All things I do thus patiently, for which
I never can requite thee but with love,   395
And that thou shalt be sure of. Thou and I
Have not been merry lately. Pray thee, tell me
Where hadst thou that same jewel in thine ear?

MARDONIUS.

Why, at the taking of a town.

ARBACES.   A wench,
Upon my life, a wench, Mardonius,   400
Gave thee that jewel.

372–373. *to interchange my bosom with*] to exchange confidences
with.

376. *in question*] in dispute.

377. *use*] profitable course of action (based on what I have said).

384. *want*] lack.

384. *parts*] qualities.

MARDONIUS.

Wench! They respect not me; I'm old and rough, and
every limb about me, but that which should, grows stiffer.
I'those businesses I may swear I am truly honest, for I
pay justly for what I take and would be glad to be at a   405
certainty.

ARBACES.

Why, do the wenches encroach upon thee?

MARDONIUS.

Ay, by this light, do they.

ARBACES.

Didst thou sit at an old rent with 'em?

MARDONIUS.

Yes, faith.   410

ARBACES.

And do they improve themselves?

MARDONIUS.

Ay, ten shillings to me every new young fellow they come
acquainted with.

ARBACES.

How canst live on't?

MARDONIUS.

Why, I think I must petition to you.   415

ARBACES.

Thou shalt take 'em up at my price.

Enter two Gentlemen *and* Bessus.

404. I'those] *Q2*; Ith those *Q1*.   416.1. *Enter . . . Bessus.*] *Q2; om.
                                              Q1.*

---

404. *honest*] (1) chaste, (2) honorable in dealing.

405–406. *to be at a certainty*] to get a fixed price; perhaps also,
punningly, to be sure of what I am getting.

407. *encroach upon thee*] demand more than they can justifiably
claim. A rent (1. 409) is said to be encroached when the lord "compels
the tenant to pay more rent than he ought" (*OED, v.* 1.b).

409. *sit at an old rent*] hold out for the old price. For the sexual
connotation of "rent," see Eric Partridge, *Shakespeare's Bawdy* (1955),
pp. 178–179.

411. *improve themselves*] (1) raise their prices, (2) better their
condition.

416. *price*] expense.

MARDONIUS.

Your price?

ARBACES.

Ay, at the king's price.

MARDONIUS.

That may be more than I am worth.

1 GENTLEMAN.

Is he not merry now?   420

2 GENTLEMAN.

I think not.

BESSUS.

He is, he is; we'll show ourselves.

ARBACES.

Bessus, I thought you had been in Iberia by this; I bade
you haste. Gobrius will want entertainment for me.

BESSUS.

An't please your majesty, I have a suit.   425

ARBACES.

Is't not lousy, Bessus? What is't?

BESSUS.

I am to carry a lady with me—

ARBACES.

Then thou hast two suits.

BESSUS.

—And if I can prefer her to the Lady Panthea, your
majesty's sister, to learn fashions, as her friends term it,   430
it will be worth something to me.

ARBACES.

So many nights' lodgings as 'tis thither, will't not?

BESSUS.

I know not that, sir, but gold I shall be sure of.

424. you haste] *Q2*; you; halfe *Q1*.   432. will't] *Q2*; will *Q1*.
429. Panthea] *Q2*; *Panthan Q1*.   433. sir] *Q2*; *om. Q1*.

---

418. *price*] value, with, perhaps, a pun on "prise" (a homophone),
the king's prise being his right to levy upon his subjects' goods for his
own use or his action of doing so. In this case, Arbaces would be telling
Mardonius facetiously that he might commandeer the wenches' services
in the king's name.

424. *want entertainment*] lack accommodations.

428. *suits*] i.e., a petition to me and a suit (of courtship) to the lady.

ARBACES.

Why, thou shalt bid her entertain her from me, so thou
wilt resolve me one thing.   435

BESSUS.

If I can.

ARBACES.

Faith, 'tis a very disputable question, and yet I think
thou canst decide it.

BESSUS.

Your majesty has a good opinion of my understanding.

ARBACES.

I have so good an opinion of it: 'tis whether thou be 440
valiant.

BESSUS.

Somebody has traduc'd me to you. Do you see this sword,
sir?   [*Draws.*]

ARBACES.

Yes.

BESSUS.

If I do not make my backbiters eat it to a knife within 445
this week, say I am not valiant.

Enter Messenger *with a packet.*

MESSENGER.

Health to your majesty!

ARBACES.   From Gobrius?

MESSENGER.   Yes, sir.

ARBACES.

How does he? Is he well?

MESSENGER.   In perfect health.

ARBACES.

Thank thee for thy good news.
A trustier servant to his prince there lives not   450
Than is good Gobrius.   [*Reads.*]

1 GENTLEMAN.

The king starts back.

437. and] *Q2; om. Q1.*   446.1. *with a packet*] *Q7; om.*
                                     Q1–6.

---

445. *backbiters*] slanderers.

MARDONIUS.   His blood goes back as fast.

2 GENTLEMAN.

    And now it comes again.

MARDONIUS.   He alters strangely.

ARBACES.

    The hand of heaven is on me; be it far

    From me to struggle. If my secret sins   455

    Have pull'd this curse upon me, lend me tears

    Enough to wash me white, that I may feel

    A childlike innocence within my breast,

    Which once perform'd, oh give me leave to stand

    As fix'd as constancy herself, my eyes   460

    Set here unmov'd, regardless of the world,

    Though thousand miseries encompass me.

MARDONIUS [*Aside*].

    This is strange.—Sir, how do you?

ARBACES.

    Mardonius, my mother—

MARDONIUS.   Is she dead?

ARBACES.

    Alas, she's not so happy. Thou dost know   465

    How she hath labor'd since my father died

    To take by treason hence this loathed life

    That would but be to serve her. I have pardon'd

    And pardon'd and by that have made her fit

    To practice new sins, not repent the old.   470

    She now has hir'd a slave to come from thence

    And strike me here, whom Gobrius, sifting out,

    Took and condemn'd and executed there,

    The careful'st servant. Heaven let me but live

    To pay that man; nature is poor to me,   475

    That will not let me have as many deaths

    As are the times that he hath sav'd my life,

    That I might die 'em over, all for him.

MARDONIUS.

    Sir, let her bear her sins on her own head;

    Vex not yourself.

---

472. *sifting out*] discovering.

ARBACES.   What will the world   480
    Conceive of me? With what unnatural sins
    Will they suppose me laden, when my life
    Is sought by her that gave it to the world?
    But yet he writes me comfort here: my sister,
    He says, is grown in beauty and in grace,   485
    In all the innocent virtues that become
    A tender, spotless maid. She stains her cheeks
    With mourning tears to purge her mother's ill,
    And 'mongst that sacred dew she mingles prayers,
    Her pure oblations for my safe return.   490
    If I have lost the duty of a son;
    If any pomp or vanity of state
    Made me forget my natural offices;
    Nay, farther, if I have not every night
    Expostulated with my wand'ring thoughts,   495
    If aught unto my parent they have err'd,
    And call'd 'em back; do you direct her arm
    Unto this foul dissembling heart of mine.
    But if I have been just to her, send out
    Your power to compass me, and hold me safe   500
    From searching treason. I will use no means
    But prayers, for rather suffer me to see
    From mine own veins issue a deadly flood
    Than wash my dangers off with mother's blood.
MARDONIUS.
    I ne'er saw such sudden extremities.   *Exeunt.* 505

[I.ii]   *Enter* Tigranes *and* Spaconia.

TIGRANES.
    Why, wilt thou have me die, Spaconia?

489. that] Q2; *her* Q1.   505. S.D. *Exeunt.*] Q2; *om.* Q1.

---

489. *that*] Q1's *her* is probably a memorial error induced by *her* in
l. 488 or l. 490.
    493. *offices*] duties.
    497. *you*] i.e., the gods.
[I.ii]
    1. *die*] Mason's notes asserted that this word should be *fly* because
Spaconia's first speech shows that "she had been exhorting [Tigranes]

What should I do?

SPACONIA.   Nay, let me stay alone;
And when you see Armenia again,
You shall behold a tomb more worth than I.
Some friend that either loves me or my cause   5
Will build me something to distinguish me
From other women. Many a weeping verse
He will lay on and much lament those maids
That place their loves unfortunately too high,
As I have done, where they can never reach.   10
But why should you go to Iberia?

TIGRANES.

Alas, that thou wilt ask me. Ask the man
That rages in a fever why he lies
Distemper'd there when all the other youths
Are coursing o'er the meadows with their loves!   15
Can I resist it? Am I not a slave
To him that conquer'd me?

SPACONIA.   That conquer'd thee?
Tigranes, he has won but half of thee,
Thy body; but thy mind may be as free
As his. His will did never combat thine   20

---

9. too high] *Weber*; too light *Q1*;   18. thee] *Q2*; *om. Q1*.
high *Q2–8, F*.

---

to flight," and the reading was adopted by Weber, who added that "the
following speech of Tigranes evidently proves the propriety of the
alteration." Subsequent editors have accepted the emendation. But
Mason apparently misinterpreted Spaconia's language; her "Nay, let me
stay alone . . ." is ironical, equivalent to "Go off to Iberia if you want
to and leave me here, but I'll be dead when you return." Nor is there
anything in Tigranes' next speech to suggest that he had thought of
flight. Instead his choices are but two: to obey Arbaces or to be
executed.

4. *more worth*] i.e., of more worth.

9. *too high*] For Q1's *too light*, most editions adopt Q2's *high*, a
reading that seems justified by the metaphor of reaching in l. 10 and
which gives a perfectly regular line. But while *high* might be misread
as *light*, it seems unlikely that it could be misread as *too light*; hence
there is a good chance, as Weber decided, that the *too* belongs in the
line, it possibly having been omitted from Q2 through a misinterpreta-
tion of the cancellation of *light* or other compositor error.

15. *coursing*] hunting.

And take it prisoner.

TIGRANES.   But if he by force
Convey my body hence, what helps it me
Or thee to be unwilling?

SPACONIA.   Oh, Tigranes,
I know you are to see a lady there,
To see and like, I fear; perhaps the hope   25
Of her makes you forget me ere we part.
Be happier than you know to wish. Farewell.

TIGRANES.
Spaconia, stay and hear me what I say.
In short, destruction meet me that I may
See it and not avoid it when I leave   30
To be thy faithful lover. Part with me
Thou shalt not. There are none that know our love,
And I have given gold to a captain
That goes unto Iberia from the king,
That he would place a lady of our land   35
With the king's sister that is offer'd me;
Thither shall you and, being once got in,
Persuade her by what subtle means you can
To be as backward in her love as I.

SPACONIA.
Can you imagine that a longing maid,   40
When she beholds you, can be pull'd away
With words from loving you?

TIGRANES.   Dispraise my health,
My honesty, and tell her I am jealous.

SPACONIA.
Why, I had rather lose you. Can my heart
Consent to let my tongue throw out such words?   45
And I, that ever yet spoke what I thought,
Shall find it such a thing at first to lie.

TIGRANES.
Yet do thy best.

---

26. me ere we part.] *Theobald*;   part, *F.*
me; ere we part *Q1–8;* me, ere we

29. *that*] so that.

Enter Bessus.

BESSUS.

What, is your majesty ready?

TIGRANES.

There is the lady, captain. 50

BESSUS.

Sweet lady, by your leave. [*Kisses her.*] I could wish my-self more full of courtship for your fair sake.

SPACONIA.

Sir, I shall find no want of that.

BESSUS.

Lady, you must haste; I have received new letters from the king that requires more speed than I expected.—He 55 will follow me suddenly himself and begins to call for your majesty already.

TIGRANES.

He shall not do so long.

BESSUS.

Sweet lady, shall I call you my charge hereafter?

SPACONIA.

I will not take upon me to govern your tongue, sir; you 60 shall call me what you please. [*Exeunt.*]

Finis Actus Primi.

[II.i]
Enter Gobrius, Bacurius, Arane, Panthea, *and waiting-women, with attendance.*

GOBRIUS.

My Lord Bacurius, you must have regard
Unto the queen. She is your prisoner;
'Tis at your peril if she make escape.

[II.i]
0.1. Panthea, *and waiting-women*] *women Q1–8, F.*
Panthæa, and Mandane, waiting

---

52. *courtship*] courtliness, gallantry.
53. *I . . . that*] i.e., I shall not miss that (because I do not desire it).

BACURIUS.
>   My lord, I know't; she is my prisoner
>   From you committed. Yet she is a woman,   5
>   And, so I keep her safe, you will not urge me
>   To keep her close. I shall not shame to say
>   I sorrow for her.
GOBRIUS.   So do I, my lord.
>   I sorrow for her that so little grace
>   Doth govern her that she should stretch her arm   10
>   Against her king, so little womanhood
>   And natural goodness as to think the death
>   Of her own son.
ARANE.   Thou know'st the reason why,
>   Dissembling as thou art, and wilt not speak.
GOBRIUS.
>   There is a lady takes not after you;   15
>   Her father is within her, that good man
>   Whose tears paid down his sins. Mark how she weeps;
>   How well it does become her. And if you
>   Can find no disposition in yourself
>   To sorrow, yet by gracefulness in her   20
>   Find out the way and by your reason weep.
>   All this she does for you, and more she needs,
>   When for yourself you will not lose a tear.
>   Think how this want of grief discredits you,
>   And you will weep because you cannot weep.   25
ARANE.
>   You talk to me as having got a time
>   Fit for your purpose, but you know I know
>   You speak not what you think.
PANTHEA.   I would my heart
>   Were stone before my softness should be urg'd
>   Against my mother. A more troubled thought   30
>   No virgin bears about her: should I excuse
>   My mother's fault, I should set light a life

6. safe,] *Q2*; safe: *Q1*.   32. set] *Q2*; let *Q1*.

---

7. *close*] confined.
17. *paid down*] immediately paid for (*OED, v.* 5.b).

In losing which a brother and a king
Were taken from me. If I seek to save
That life so lov'd, I lose another life   35
That gave me being—I shall lose a mother,
A word of such a sound in a child's ear
That it strikes reverence through it. May the will
Of heaven be done, and, if one needs must fall,
Take a poor virgin's life to answer all.   40

ARANE.

But Gobrius, let us talk.   [*They walk apart.*]
                    You know this fault
Is not in me as in another woman.

GOBRIUS.

I know it is not.

ARANE.   Yet you make it so.

GOBRIUS.

Why, is not all that's past beyond your help?

ARANE.

I know it is.

GOBRIUS.   Nay, should you publish it   45
Before the world, think you 'twill be believ'd?

ARANE.

I know it would not.

GOBRIUS.   Nay, should I join with you,
Should we not both be torn? And yet both die
Uncredited?

ARANE.   I think we should.

GOBRIUS.   Why then
Take you such violent courses? As for me,   50
I do but right in saving of the king
From all your plots.

ARANE.   The king?

GOBRIUS.   I bade you rest
With patience, and a time would come for me
To reconcile all to your own content.
But by this way you take away my power,   55
And what was done unknown was not by me
But you. Your urging being done,

---

48. *torn*] torn to pieces.

I must preserve mine own; but time may bring
All this to light and happily for all.

ARANE.

Accursed be this over-curious brain   60
That gave that plot a birth; accurst this womb
That after did conceive to my disgrace.

BACURIUS.

My Lord Protector, they say there are divers letters come
from Armenia that Bessus has done good service and
brought again a day by his particular valor. Receiv'd you   65
any to that effect?

GOBRIUS.

Yes, 'tis most certain.

BACURIUS.

I'm sorry for't, not that the day was won but that 'twas
won by him. We held him here a coward; he did me
wrong once at which I laugh'd and so did all the world,   70
for nor I nor any other held him worth my sword.

Enter Bessus *and* Spaconia.

BESSUS.

Health to my Lord Protector! From the king these letters
—and to your grace, madam, these.

GOBRIUS.

How does his majesty?

BESSUS.

As well as conquest by his own means, and his valiant   75
commanders', can make him. Your letters will tell you all.

PANTHEA.

I will not open mine till I do know
My brother's health; good captain, is he well?

BESSUS.

As the rest of us that fought are.

71. him] *Q2*; time *Q1*.

60. *over-curious*] too-ingenious.   63. *divers*] several.
65. *brought again*] recovered.
71. *him*] Q1 also confuses initial *h* for *t* at II.i.227, IV.i.67, and
IV.ii.199.

PANTHEA.

But how's that? Is he hurt?   80

BESSUS.

He's a strange soldier that gets not a knock.

PANTHEA.

I do not ask how strange that soldier is
That gets no hurt, but whether he have one.

BESSUS.

He had divers.

PANTHEA.

And is he well again?   85

BESSUS.

Well again, an't please your grace? Why, I was run twice
through the body and shot i'th' head with a cross arrow
and yet am well again.

PANTHEA.

I do not care how thou dost. Is he well?

BESSUS.

Not care how I do! Let a man out of the mightiness of   90
his spirit fructify foreign countries with his blood for the
good of his own, and thus he shall be answered. Why, I
may live to relieve with spear and shield such a lady as
you distressed.

PANTHEA.

Why, I will care; I am glad that thou art well.   95
I prithee, is he so?

GOBRIUS.

The king is well and will be here tomorrow.

PANTHEA.

My prayers are heard; now I will open mine.   [*Reads.*]

GOBRIUS.

Bacurius, I must ease you of your charge.—
Madam, the wonted mercy of the king,   100
That overtakes your faults, has met with this

93–94. as you] *Q2*; *om. Q1.*

---

84. *divers*] several.
87. *cross arrow*] crossbow bolt.
100. *wonted*] accustomed.
101. *overtakes*] exceeds.

And struck it out; he has forgiven you freely.
Your own will is your law; be where you please.

ARANE.

I thank him.

GOBRIUS.   You will be ready to wait
Upon his majesty tomorrow?

ARANE.   I will.   105

BACURIUS.

Madam, be wise hereafter. I am glad
I have lost this office.   *Exit* Arane.

GOBRIUS.

Good Captain Bessus, tell us the discourse
Between Tigranes and our king and how
We got the victory.

PANTHEA.   I prithee do,   110
And if my brother were in any danger,
Let not thy tale make him abide there long
Before thou bring him off, for all that while
My heart will beat.

BESSUS.

Madam, let what will beat, I must tell the truth, and   115
thus it was. They fought single in lists but one to one.
As for my own part, I was dangerously hurt but three
days before, else perhaps we had been two to two—I cannot tell; some thought we had. And the occasion of my
hurt was this: the enemy had made trenches—   120

GOBRIUS.

Captain, without the manner of your hurt
Be much material to this business,
We'll hear it some other time.

PANTHEA.   Ay, I prithee
Leave it, and go on with my brother.

BESSUS.

I will, but 'twould be worth your hearing. To the lists   125

107. S.D. Arane] *Q2; om. Q1.*   115. the] *Q2; om. Q1.*

---

108. *discourse*] intercourse (rather than conversation).
121. *without*] unless.
125. *lists*] fighting area (cf. I.i.20).

they came, and single sword and gauntlet was their fight.

PANTHEA.

Alas!

BESSUS.

Without the lists there stood some dozen captains of
either side mingled, all which were sworn, and one of
those was I. And 'twas my chance to stand near a captain 130
of the enemy's side called Tiribasus; valiant they said he
was. Whilst these two kings were stretching themselves,
this Tiribasus cast something a scornful look on me and
ask'd me whom I thought would overcome. I smil'd and
told him if he would fight with me he should perceive by 135
the event of that whose king would win. Something he
answered, and a scuffle was like to grow, when one Zipetus
offer'd to help him. I—

PANTHEA.

All this is of thyself; I prithee, Bessus,
Tell something of my brother. Did he nothing?   140

BESSUS.

Why, yes; I'll tell your grace. They were not to fight till
the word given, which, for my own part, by my troth, I
confess I was not to give.

PANTHEA.

See, for his own part.

BACURIUS.

I fear yet this fellow's abus'd with a good report.   145

BESSUS.

Ay, but I—

PANTHEA.

Still of himself.

142–143. I confess] Q2; om. Q1.

_____

126. *single sword and gauntlet*] One who fought single sword was
armed with the sword only and did not carry other offensive or defen-
sive weapons, such as the dagger, the cloak, or the buckler. The gauntlet, a mailed glove, was worn on the hand not engaged with the sword
and furnished protection when one tried to catch his opponent's blade.
According to *Vincentio Saviolo, His Practise,* a manual of swordsman-
ship published in 1595, "the single Swoorde and the glove" was the
style then "most in use among Gentlemen" (F3ᵛ).

BESSUS.

    —Cried, "Give the word," whenas, some of them said,
Tigranes was stooping, but the word was not given then,
when one Cosroes, of the enemy's part, held up his finger 150
to me, which is as much with us martialists as "I will
fight with you." I said not a word nor made sign during
the combat, but that once done—

PANTHEA.

    He slips o'er all the fight.

BESSUS.

    —I call'd him to me. "Cosroes," said I—   155

PANTHEA.

    I will hear no more.

BESSUS.

    —No, no, I lie—

BACURIUS.

    I dare be sworn thou dost.

BESSUS.

    —"Captain," said I; 'twas so.

PANTHEA.

    I tell thee, I will hear no further.   160

BESSUS.

    No? Your grace will wish you had.

PANTHEA.

    I will not wish it. What, is this the lady
My brother writes to me to take?

BESSUS.

    An't please your grace, this is she.—Charge, will you come
nearer the princess?   165

PANTHEA.

    Y'are welcome from your country, and this land
Shall show unto you all the kindnesses
That I can make it. What's your name?

SPACONIA.   Thalestris.

---

148. whenas,] when as *Q1–8, F.*

---

    148. *whenas*] at the time at which. Modern editions usually punc-
tuate *when, as* and in 1. 150 adopt Q2's *yet* for Q1's *when* in order to
avoid the repetition.

PANTHEA.

    Y'are very welcome; you have got a letter
    To put you to me that has power enough   170
    To place mine enemy here, then much more you
    That are so far from being so to me
    That you ne'er saw me.

BESSUS.

    Madam, I dare pass my word for her truth.

SPACONIA.

    My truth!   175

PANTHEA.

    Why, captain, do you think I am afraid she'll steal?

BESSUS.

    I cannot tell—servants are slippery—but I dare give my
word for her and for her honesty. She came along with
me and many favors she did me by the way, but, by this
light, none but what she might do with modesty to a 180
man of my rank.

PANTHEA.

    Why, captain, here's nobody thinks otherwise.

BESSUS.

    Nay, if you should, your grace may think your pleasure.
But I am sure I brought her from Armenia, and in all
that way, if ever I touch'd any bare on her above her 185
knee, I pray God I may sink where I stand.

SPACONIA.

    Above my knee!

BESSUS.

    No, you know I did not, and if any man will say I did,
this sword shall answer. Nay, I'll defend the reputation
of my charge whilst I live.—Your grace shall understand 190
I am secret in these businesses and know how to defend
a lady's honor.

SPACONIA.

    I hope your grace knows him so well already,
    I shall not need to tell you he's vain and foolish.

---

    174. *truth*] (1) virtue, (2) uprightness and integrity. Panthea (1. 176)
understands the second sense.
    178. *honesty*] (1) integrity, (2) chastity.

BESSUS.

    Ay, you may call me what you please, but I'll defend   195
your good name against the world.—And so I take my
leave of your grace—and of you, my Lord Protector. I am
likewise glad to see your lordship well.

BACURIUS.

    Oh, Captain Bessus, I thank you; I would speak with you
anon.   200

BESSUS.

    When you please, I will attend your lordship.   *Exit.*

BACURIUS.

    Madam, I'll take my leave too.

PANTHEA.   Good Bacurius.   *Exit* [Bacurius].

GOBRIUS.

    Madam, what writes his majesty to you?

PANTHEA.

    Oh, my lord,
The kindest words; I'll keep 'em whilst I live,   205
Here in my bosom. There's no art in 'em;
They lie disorder'd in this paper just
As hearty nature speaks 'em.

GOBRIUS.   And to me
He writes what tears of joy he shed to hear
How you were grown in every virtuous way,   210
And yields all thanks to me for that dear care
Which I was bound to have in training you.
There is no princess living that enjoys
A brother of that worth.

PANTHEA.   My lord, no maid
Longs more for anything or feels more heat   215
And cold within her breast than I do now
In hope to see him.

GOBRIUS.   Yet I wonder much
At this: he writes he brings along with him
A husband for you, that same captive prince.
And if he love you as he makes a show,   220

202. S.D. *Exit.*] *after* too *Q1–2,   Bacurius. F.*
7–8; om. Q3–6; Exeunt Bessus and

---

200. *anon*] immediately.

He will allow you freedom in your choice.

PANTHEA.

And so he will, my lord; I warrant you
He will but offer and give me the power
To take or leave.

GOBRIUS.   Trust me, were I a lady,
I could not like that man were bargain'd with   225
Before I choose him.

PANTHEA.   But I am not built
On such wild humors; if I find him worthy,
He is not less because he's offer'd.

SPACONIA [Aside].

'Tis true, he is not; would he would seem less.

GOBRIUS.

I think there is no lady can affect   230
Another prince, your brother standing by;
He does eclipse men's virtues so with his.

SPACONIA [Aside].

I know a lady may; and more, I fear
Another lady will.

PANTHEA.   Would I might see him.

GOBRIUS.

Why, so you shall. My businesses are great;   235
I will attend you when it is his pleasure
To see you, madam.

PANTHEA.   I thank you, good my lord.

GOBRIUS.

You will be ready, madam?

PANTHEA.

Yes.   Exit Gobrius [attended].

SPACONIA.

I do beseech you, madam, send away   240
Your other women and receive from me
A few sad words, which set against your joys
May make 'em shine the more.

---

227. him] Q2; time Q1.   239. S.D. Exit Gobrius.] after mad-
232. his] Q2; this Q1.   am? Q2–8, F; Exit. after madam?
                                  Q1.

226–227. built . . . humors] of such a capricious disposition.
227. him] Cf. II.i.71.   242. sad] grave, serious.

PANTHEA.   Sirs, leave me all.   *Exeunt women.*

SPACONIA.

     I kneel a stranger here to beg a thing
     Unfit for me to ask and you to grant;   245
     'Tis such another strange, ill-laid request
     As if a beggar should intreat a king
     To leave his scepter and his throne to him
     And take his rags to wander o'er the world
     Hungry and cold.

PANTHEA.   That were a strange request.   250

SPACONIA.

     As ill is mine.

PANTHEA.   Then do not utter it.

SPACONIA.

     Alas, 'tis of that nature that it must
     Be utter'd—ay, and granted—or I die.
     I am asham'd to speak it; but where life
     Lies at the stake, I cannot think her woman   255
     That will not talk something unreasonably
     To hazard saving of it. I shall seem
     A strange petitioner, that wish all ill
     To them I beg of ere they give me aught,
     Yet so I must. I would you were not fair   260
     Nor wise, for in your ill consists my good.
     If you were foolish, you would hear my prayer;
     If foul, you had not power to hinder me—
     He would not love you.

PANTHEA.   What's the meaning of it?

SPACONIA.

     Nay, my request is more without the bounds   265
     Of reason yet, for 'tis not in the power
     Of you to do what I would have you grant.

PANTHEA.

     Why, then, 'tis idle. Prithee speak it out.

---

243. S.D. *Exeunt women.*] Q2; *om.*   256. talk] *Theobald*; take Q1–8, F.
Q1.

---

    243. *Sirs*] a term of address appropriate to ladies as well as
gentlemen.
    256. *something*] somewhat.

SPACONIA.

    Your brother brings a prince into this land
    Of such a noble shape, so sweet a grace,   270
    So full of worth withal, that every maid
    That looks upon him gives away herself
    To him forever, and for you to have
    He brings him. And so mad is my demand
    That I desire you not to have this man,   275
    This excellent man, for whom you needs must die
    If you should miss him. I do now expect
    You should laugh at me.

PANTHEA.   Trust me, I could weep
    Rather, for I have found in all thy words
    A strange, disjointed sorrow.

SPACONIA.   'Tis by me   280
    His own desire too that you would not love him.

PANTHEA.

    His own desire! Why, credit me, Thalestris,
    I am no common wooer. If he shall woo me,
    His worth may be such that I dare not swear
    I will not love him, but if he will stay   285
    To have me woo him, I will promise thee
    He may keep all his graces to himself
    And fear no ravishing from me.

SPACONIA.   'Tis yet
    His own desire, but when he sees your face,
    I fear it will not be. Therefore, I charge you   290
    As you have pity, stop those tender ears
    From his enchanting voice, close up those eyes
    That you may neither catch a dart from him
    Nor he from you. I charge you as you hope
    To live in quiet, for when I am dead   295
    For certain I shall walk to visit him
    If he break promise with me, for as fast
    As oaths, without a formal ceremony,
    Can make me, I am to him.

PANTHEA.   Then be fearless,

---

271. *withal*] besides.
296. *walk*] rise from my grave.

For if he were a thing 'twixt god and man   300
I could gaze on him, if I knew it sin
To love him, without passion. Dry your eyes.
I swear you shall enjoy him still for me;
I will not hinder you. But I perceive
You are not what you seem; rise, rise, Thalestris,   305
If your right name be so.
SPACONIA.   Indeed, it is not.
Spaconia is my name, but I desire
Not to be known to others.
PANTHEA.   Why, by me
You shall not. I will never do you wrong;
What good I can, I will. Think not my birth   310
Or education such that I should injure
A stranger virgin. You are welcome hither.
In company you wish to be commanded,
But when we are alone, I shall be ready
To be your servant.   *Exeunt.* 315

[II.ii]   *Enter three* Men *and a* Woman.

1 MAN.
Come, come, run, run, run.
2 MAN.
We shall outgo her.
3 MAN.
One were better be hang'd than carry women out fiddling
to these shows.
WOMAN.
Is the king hard by?   5
1 MAN.
You heard he with the bottles say he thought we should
come too late. What abundance of people here is.

307. my] *Q2; om. Q1.*   315. S.D. *Exeunt.*] *Q2; Exit. Q1.*

---

303. *still for me*] always as far as I am concerned.
312. *stranger*] foreign.
[II.ii]
3. *fiddling*] skylarking, wasting time.
5. *hard by*] at hand.

WOMAN.

But what had he in those bottles?

3 MAN.

I know not.

2 MAN.

Why, ink, goodman fool.   10

3 MAN.

Ink! What to do?

1 MAN.

Why, the king, look you, will many times call for those
bottles and break his mind to his friends.

WOMAN.

Let's take our places quickly; we shall have no room else.

2 MAN.

The man told us he would walk afoot through the   15
people.

3 MAN.

Ay, marry, did he.

1 MAN.

Our shops are well look'd to now.

2 MAN.

'Slife, yonder's my master, I think.

1 MAN.

No, 'tis not he.   20

Enter two Citizens' Wives *and* Philip.

1 CITIZEN'S WIFE.

Lord, how fine the fields be. What sweet living 'tis in the
country.

2 CITIZEN'S WIFE.

Ay, poor souls, God help 'em; they live as contentedly as
one of us.

1 CITIZEN'S WIFE.

My husband's cousin would have had me gone into the   25
country last year. Wert thou ever there?

2 CITIZEN'S WIFE.

Ay, poor souls, I was amongst 'em once.

18. look'd] *Q2;* looke *Q1.*

1 CITIZEN'S WIFE.
    And what kind of creatures are they, for love of God?
2 CITIZEN'S WIFE.
    Very good people, God help 'em.
1 CITIZEN'S WIFE.
    Wilt thou go with me down this summer, when I am   30
    brought abed?
2 CITIZEN'S WIFE.
    Alas, 'tis no place for us.
1 CITIZEN'S WIFE.
    Why, prithee?
2 CITIZEN'S WIFE.
    Why, you can have nothing there; there's nobody cries
    brooms.   35
1 CITIZEN'S WIFE.
    No!
2 CITIZEN'S WIFE.
    No, truly, nor milk.
1 CITIZEN'S WIFE.
    Nor milk? How do they?
2 CITIZEN'S WIFE.
    They are fain to milk themselves i'th' country.
1 CITIZEN'S WIFE.
    Good Lord! But the people there, I think, will be very   40
    dutiful to one of us?
2 CITIZEN'S WIFE.
    Ay, God knows, will they, and yet they do not greatly care
    for our husbands.
1 CITIZEN'S WIFE.
    Do they not, alas? In good faith, I cannot blame them,
    for we do not greatly care for them ourselves.—Philip, I   45
    pray choose us a place.
PHILIP.
    There's the best, forsooth.
1 CITIZEN'S WIFE.
    By your leave, good people, a little.

---

39. *fain*] obliged.

3 MAN.

What's the matter?

PHILIP.

I pray you, my friend, do not thrust my mistress so; she's   50
with child.

2 MAN.

Let her look to herself then; has she not had shroving
enough yet? If she stay shouldering here, she may hap to
go home with a cake in her belly.

3 MAN.

How now, goodman squitter-breech; why do you lean so   55
on me?

PHILIP.

Because I will.

3 MAN.

Will you, sir sauce-box?   [*Strikes him.*]

1 CITIZEN'S WIFE.

Look if one have not struck Philip.—Come hither, Philip;
why did he strike thee?   60

PHILIP.

For leaning on him.

1 CITIZEN'S WIFE.

Why didst thou lean on him?

---

49. S.P. 3 MAN.] *Q2*; 1. *Q1*.   52. shroving] showing *Q2–6*, *F.;*
50. you] *Q2*; *om. Q1*.   shroving *Q7–8*; thrusting *Q1*.

---

52. *shroving*] merrymaking, from the festivity associated with Shrove-
tide. Cf. *The Noble Gentleman*, III.ii: ". . . 'twill be rarely strange/ To
see him stated thus, as though he went/ A-shroving through the city.
. . ." The Q1 reading is probably a memorial error induced by *thrust*
in l. 50; the Q2 reading probably resulted from the compositor's misreading of a correct annotation in his copy.

53. *hap*] chance.

54. *cake*] Pancakes were traditionally served on Shrove Tuesday, and
cake generally symbolized festivity and gaiety (cf. Sir Toby's "Dost think
because thou art virtuous, there shall be no more cakes and ale?"
Twelfth Night, II.iii). The Second Man probably means something like
"If she tries to push me around, she's likely to go home with even
more of the fruits of merrymaking in her womb (belly) than she already
carries."

55. *squitter-breech*] one afflicted with diarrhea.

PHILIP.

I did not think he would have struck me.

1 CITIZEN'S WIFE.

As God save me, law, thou art as wild as a buck; there is
no quarrel but thou art at one end or other of it.   65

3 MAN.

It's at the first end then, for he will never stay the last.

1 CITIZEN'S WIFE.

Well, slipstring, I shall meet with you.

3 MAN.

When you will.

1 CITIZEN'S WIFE.

I'll give a crown to meet with you.

3 MAN.

At a bawdy house.   70

1 CITIZEN'S WIFE.

Ay, you are full of your roguery—[aside] but if I do meet
you, it shall cost me a fall.

3 MAN.

The king, the king, the king, the king! Now, now, now,
now!

Enter Arbaces, Tigranes, Mardonius, _and others._

ALL.

God preserve your majesty!   75

67. slipstring] _Q2_; stripling _Q1_.

---

67. _slipstring_] rogue, one who deserves hanging (_OED_).

67. _meet with_] get even with. But the Third Man (l. 70) shifts the
meaning to "encounter."

73–74. 3 MAN. _The . . . now!_] Q2 precedes this speech with the stage
direction _Flourish, Enter one running._ and assigns the speech itself to _4_,
that is, the man who enters. It is difficult to know which text to follow.
Although the _Flourish_ is doubtless the prompter's addition, it is possible
that a stage direction and new speech prefix stood in the authors'
papers. If the direction was omitted by the copyist, which is not
unlikely in view of what seem to be his other omissions, the Q1 compositor may then have altered the _4_ to _3_. On the other hand, there is
nothing really wrong with the Q1 action; the Third Man may simply
look off stage during the speech of the First Citizen's Wife and, seeing
the kings, cry out in excitement. Thus it seems safer to follow Q1, for
if the _Flourish_ is of non-authorial origin, the other Q2 changes closely
associated with it may be too.

ARBACES.

    I thank you all. Now are my joys at full,
    When I behold you safe, my loving subjects.
    By you I grow; 'tis your united love
    That lifts me to this height.
    All the account that I can render you   80
    For all the love you have bestowed on me,
    All your expenses to maintain my war,
    Is but a little word. You will imagine
    'Tis slender payment, yet 'tis such a word
    As is not to be bought without our bloods: 85
    'Tis peace.

ALL.   God preserve your majesty!

ARBACES.

    Now you may live securely in your towns,
    Your children 'round about you; you may sit
    Under your vines and make the miseries
    Of other kingdoms a discourse for you   90
    And lend them sorrows. For yourselves, you may
    Safely forget there are such things as tears,
    And may you all whose good thoughts I have gain'd
    Hold me unworthy when I think my life
    A sacrifice too great to keep you thus   95
    In such a calm estate.

ALL.   God bless your majesty!

ARBACES.

    See, all good people, I have brought the man
    Whose very name you fear'd a captive home.
    Behold him; 'tis Tigranes. In your hearts
    Sing songs of gladness and deliverance.   100

1 CITIZEN'S WIFE.

    Out upon him!

2 CITIZEN'S WIFE.

    How he looks!

WOMAN.

    Hang him, hang him, hang him!

103. S.P. WOMAN.] *Dyce*; 3 *Weo.*
Q1–8, F.

MARDONIUS.

　　These are sweet people.

TIGRANES.　　　　　　　　Sir, you do me wrong

　　To render me a scorned spectacle　　　　　　　　　105

　　To common people.

ARBACES.　　　　　　It was far from me

　　To mean it so.—If I have aught deserv'd,

　　My loving subjects, let me beg of you

　　Not to revile this prince, in whom there dwells

　　All worth of which the nature of a man　　　　　　110

　　Is capable, valor beyond compare.

　　The terror of his name has stretch'd itself

　　Wherever there is sun. And yet for you

　　I fought with him single and won him too;

　　I made his valor stoop and brought that name,　　115

　　Soar'd to so unbeliev'd a height, to fall

　　Beneath mine. This, inspir'd with all your loves,

　　I did perform; and will, for your content,

　　Be ever ready for a greater work.

ALL.

　　The Lord bless your majesty.

TIGRANES [Aside].　　　　　　So, he has made me　　120

　　Amends now with a speech in commendations

　　Of himself. I would not be so vainglorious.

ARBACES.

　　If there be anything in which I may

　　Do good to any creature, here speak out;

　　For I must leave you, and it troubles me　　　　　　125

　　Thus my occasions for the good of you

　　Are such as calls me from you, else my joy

　　Would be to spend my days amongst you all.

　　You show your loves in these large multitudes

　　That come to meet me. I will pray for you;　　　　130

　　Heaven prosper you that you may know old years

115. brought] Q2; made Q1.

---

　　114. *won*] overcame.

　　115. *brought*] caused. The Q1 reading is probably a memorial error induced by *made* earlier in the line.

　　116. *unbeliev'd*] incredible.

And live to see your children's children
Eat at your boards with plenty. When there is
A want of anything, let it be known
To me, and I will be a father to you.   135
God keep you all.

ALL.

God bless your majesty! God bless your majesty!
                          Exeunt kings and their train.

1 MAN.

Come, shall we go? All's done.

WOMAN.

Ay, for God's sake; I have not made a fire yet.

2 MAN.

Away, away; all's done.   140

3 MAN.

Content.—Farewell, Philip.

1 CITIZEN'S WIFE.

Away, you haltersack you.

2 MAN.

Philip will not fight; he's afraid on's face.

PHILIP.

Ay, marry, am I afraid of my face.

3 MAN.

Thou wouldst be, Philip, if thou saw'st it in a glass; it 145
looks so like a visor.

1 CITIZEN'S WIFE.

You'll be hang'd, sirrah. [*Exeunt the three* Men *and the*
Woman.] Come, Philip, walk afore us homeward.—Did
not his majesty say he had brought us home peas for all
our money?   150

137. God . . . majesty!] *Q2; repe-*   147–148. S.D. *Exeunt . . . Woman.*]
tition om. Q1.   *Exeunt 1, 2, 3, and Women. Q1;*
137.1. *Exeunt . . . train.*] *after* all, *Exeunt 2. 3. and Women. Q2–4,*
l. 136 Q2–8, F; Exeunt. after all   *7–8; . . . 2. 3. and woman. Q5–6, F*
Q1.   *(all after l. 146).*
143. S.P. 2 MAN.] *Q2;* 1. *Q1.*   149. all] *Q2; om. Q1.*
146. so] *Q2; om. Q1.*

142. *haltersack*] gallows-bird.
143. *on's*] for his.
146. *visor*] vizard, mask.

2 CITIZEN'S WIFE.

    Yes, marry, did he.

1 CITIZEN'S WIFE.

    They are the first I heard on this year, by my troth. I
long'd for some of 'em; did he not say we should have
some?

2 CITIZEN'S WIFE.

    Yes, and so we shall anon, I warrant you, have every one 155
a peck brought home to our houses.   *[Exeunt.]*

Finis Actus Secundi.

[III.i]   *Enter* Arbaces *and* Gobrius.

ARBACES.

    My sister take it ill?

GOBRIUS.   Not very ill;

Something unkindly she doth take it, sir,

To have her husband chosen to her hands.

ARBACES.

    Why, Gobrius, let her; I must have her know

My will, and not her own, must govern her.   5

What, will she marry with some slave at home?

GOBRIUS.

    Oh, she is far from any stubbornness—

You much mistake her—and no doubt will like

Where you will have her; but when you behold her,

You will be loath to part with such a jewel.   10

ARBACES.

    To part with her! Why, Gobrius, art thou mad?

She is my sister.

GOBRIUS.   Sir, I know she is,

But it were pity to make poor our land

With such a beauty to enrich another.

---

    152. *on*] of.

    155. *anon*] immediately.

[III.1]

    2. *Something unkindly*] somewhat unfavorably.

    3. *to her hands*] without consent or action on her part.

    6. *slave*] contemptible person.

ARBACES.

    Pish! Will she have him?

GOBRIUS [*Aside*].   I do hope she will not.—   15

    I think she will, sir.

ARBACES.

    Were she my father and my mother too

    And all the names for which we think folks friends,

    She should be forc'd to have him when I know

    'Tis fit. I will not hear her say she's loath.   20

GOBRIUS [*Aside*].

    Heaven bring my purpose luckily to pass;

    You know 'tis just.—Sir, she'll not need constraint,

    She loves you so.

ARBACES.   How does she love me? Speak.

GOBRIUS.

    She loves you more than people love their health

    That live by labor, more than I could love   25

    A man that died for me if he could live

    Again.

ARBACES.   She is not like her mother then?

GOBRIUS.

    Oh, no; when you were in Armenia,

    I durst not let her know when you were hurt,

    For at the first on every little scratch,   30

    She kept her chamber, wept, and would not eat,

    Till you were well. And many times the news

    Was so long coming that before we heard

    She was as near her death as you your health.

ARBACES.

    Alas, poor soul; but yet she must be rul'd.   35

    I know not how I shall requite her well.

    I long to see her; have you sent for her

    To tell her I am ready?

GOBRIUS.   Sir, I have.

Enter 1 Gentleman *and* Tigranes.

15. I do . . . not] *Q2*; *om. Q1*.   38.1. 1 Gentleman *and*] *Q2*; *om.*
                                         Q1.

1 GENTLEMAN.
    Sir, here's the Armenian king.
ARBACES.   He's welcome.
1 GENTLEMAN.
    And the queen-mother and the princess wait without.   40
ARBACES.
    Good Gobrius bring them in.   [*Exit* Gobrius.]
                      Tigranes, you
    Will think you are arriv'd in a strange land,
    Where mothers cast to poison their only sons;
    Think you, you shall be safe?
TIGRANES.   Too safe I am, sir.

Enter Gobrius, Arane, Panthea, Spaconia, Bacurius, Mardonius,
2 Gentleman, *and* Bessus.

ARANE.
    As low as this I bow to you and would   45
    As low as is my grave to show a mind
    Thankful for all your mercies.
ARBACES.   Oh, stand up
    And let me kneel; the light will be asham'd
    To see observance done to me by you.
ARANE.
    You are my king.
ARBACES.   You are my mother; rise.   50
    As far be all your faults from your own soul
    As from my memory; then you shall be
    As white as innocence herself.
ARANE.   I came
    Only to show my duty and acknowledge
    My sorrow for my sins; longer to stay   55

---

39. *and* 40. S.P. 1 GENTLEMAN.] *Q2;*   *and Bessus, and two Gentlemen*
Gent. Q1.   *Q2–6, F; and Bessus Q1.*
44.2. 2 Gentleman, *and* Bessus]   46. is] *Q2;* to *Q1.*

---

    43. *cast*] plot, devise.
    44. *Too safe*] too confined, secure.
    46. *is*] Q1's *to* is probably a memorial error induced by *to* in l. 45
or later in l. 46.

Were but to draw eyes more attentively
Upon my shame. That power that kept you safe
From me preserve you still.

ARBACES.   Your own desires
Shall be your guard.   *Exit* Arane.

PANTHEA.   Now let me die;
Since I have seen my lord the king return   60
In safety, I have seen all good that life
Can show me. I have ne'er another wish
For Heaven to grant, nor were it fit I should,
For I am bound to spend my age to come
In giving thanks that this was granted me.   65

GOBRIUS.
Why does not your majesty speak?

ARBACES.
To whom?

GOBRIUS.
To the princess.

PANTHEA.
Alas, sir, I am fearful; you do look
On me as if I were some loathed thing   70
That you were finding out a way to shun.

GOBRIUS.
Sir, you should speak to her.

ARBACES.
Ha?

PANTHEA.
I know I am unworthy, yet not ill
Arm'd, with which innocence here I will kneel   75
Till I am one with earth, but I will gain
Some words and kindness from you.

TIGRANES.
Will you speak, sir?

ARBACES [*Aside*].   Speak! Am I what I was?
What art thou that dost creep into my breast
And dar'st not see my face? Show forth thyself.   80

59. S.D. *Exit* Arane.] *Q2*; *Exit. after* still, *l. 58 Q1.*

I feel a pair of fiery wings display'd
Hither, from thence. You shall not tarry there;
Up and begone. If thou beest love, begone,
Or I will tear thee from my wounded flesh,
Pull thy lov'd down away, and with a quill,   85
By this right arm drawn from thy wanton wing,
Write to thy laughing mother in thy blood
That you are powers belied and all your darts
Are to be blown away by men resolv'd
Like dust. I know thou fear'st my words; away.   90

TIGRANES [*Aside*].
Oh, misery, why should he be so slow?
There can no falsehood come of loving her,
Though I have given my faith; she is a thing
Both to be lov'd and serv'd beyond my faith.
I would he would present me to her quickly.   95

PANTHEA.
Will you not speak at all? Are you so far
From kind words? Yet to save my modesty,
That must talk till you answer, do not stand
As you were dumb; say something, though it be
Poison'd with anger that may strike me dead.   100

MARDONIUS.
Have you no life at all? For manhood sake,
Let her not kneel and talk neglected thus.
A tree would find a tongue to answer her,
Did she but give it such a lov'd respect.

ARBACES.
You mean this lady? Lift her from the earth;   105
Why do you let her kneel so long?—Alas,
Madam, your beauty uses to command
And not to beg; what is your suit to me?
It shall be granted; yet the time is short
And my affairs are great.—But where's my sister?   110
I bade she should be brought.

MARDONIUS [*Aside*].   What, is he mad?

ARBACES.
Gobrius, where is she?

---

104. *respect*] attention, regard.

GOBRIUS.

    Sir?

ARBACES.

    Where is she, man?

GOBRIUS.

    Who, sir? 115

ARBACES.

    Who? Hast thou forgot? My sister.

GOBRIUS.

    Your sister, sir?

ARBACES.

    Your sister, sir? Someone that has a wit

    Answer; where is she?

GOBRIUS.   Do you not see her there?

ARBACES.

    Where? 120

GOBRIUS.

    There.

ARBACES.

    There? Where?

MARDONIUS.

    'Slight, there; are you blind?

ARBACES.

    Which do you mean? That little one?   [*Indicates* Spaconia.]

GOBRIUS.   No, sir.

ARBACES.

    No, sir! Why do you mock me? I can see 125

    No other here but that petitioning lady.

GOBRIUS.

    That's she.

ARBACES.   Away.

GOBRIUS.   Sir, it is she.

ARBACES.   'Tis false—

GOBRIUS.

    Is it?

118–122. ARBACES. Your ... Where?] she?/ *Arb.* Do . . . there?/ *Gob.*
Q2; Q1 assigns as follows: Arb. Where?/ *Arb.* There./ *Gob.*
Your . . . sir?/ *Gob.* Someone . . . There? Where?

123. *'Slight*] a common ejaculation; literally, "by God's light."

ARBACES. —As hell; by heaven, as false as hell!
　　　My sister—is she dead? If it be so,
　　　Speak boldly to me, for I am a man　　　　　　　　130
　　　And dare not quarrel with divinity,
　　　But do not think to cozen me with this.
　　　I see you all are mute and stand amaz'd,
　　　Fearful to answer me; it is too true
　　　A decreed instant cuts off every life,　　　　　　135
　　　For which to mourn is to repine. She died
　　　A virgin though, more innocent than sleep,
　　　As clear as her own eyes, and blessedness
　　　Eternal waits upon her where she is.
　　　I know she could not make a wish to change　　　140
　　　Her state for new, and you shall see me bear
　　　My crosses like a man. We all must die,
　　　And she hath taught us how.
GOBRIUS.　　　　　　　　　　　Do not mistake
　　　And vex yourself for nothing, for her death
　　　Is a long life off yet, I hope. 'Tis she;　　　　　145
　　　And if my speech deserve not faith, lay death
　　　Upon me, and my latest words shall force
　　　A credit from you.
ARBACES.　　　　　　　Which, good Gobrius?
　　　That lady dost thou mean?
GOBRIUS.　　　　　　　　　　That lady, sir.
　　　She is your sister, and she is your sister　　　　150
　　　That loves you so; 'tis she for whom I weep
　　　To see you use her thus.
ARBACES.　　　　　　　　It cannot be.
TIGRANES [*Aside*]. Pish, this is tedious.
　　　I cannot hold; I must present myself.
　　　And yet the sight of my Spaconia　　　　　　　155
　　　Touches me as a sudden thunderclap
　　　Does one that is about to sin.

150–152. She . . . thus.] *Q2; om. Q1.*

---

　　132. *cozen*] deceive.
　　139. *waits upon*] accompanies, or, perhaps, more specifically, attends
in the manner of a servant.
　　147. *latest*] last.

ARBACES.   Away;
   No more of this. Here I pronounce him traitor,
   The direct plotter of my death, that names
   Or thinks her for my sister. 'Tis a lie,   160
   The most malicious of the world, invented
   To mad your king; he that will say so next,
   Let him draw out his sword and sheath it here—
   It is a sin fully as pardonable.
   She is no kin to me nor shall she be;   165
   If she were any, I create her none,
   And which of you can question this? My power
   Is like the sea, that is to be obey'd
   And not disputed with. I have decreed her
   As far from having part of blood with me   170
   As the nak'd Indians. Come and answer me,
   He that is boldest now: is that my sister?
MARDONIUS [*Aside*].
   Oh, this is fine.
BESSUS.
   No, marry, is she not, an't please your majesty.
   I never thought she was; she's nothing like you.   175
ARBACES.
   No; 'tis true, she is not.
MARDONIUS [*To* Bessus].   Thou shouldst be hang'd.
PANTHEA.
   Sir, I will speak but once. By the same power
   You make my blood a stranger unto yours,
   You may command me dead, and, so much love
   A stranger may importune, pray you, do.   180
   If this request appear too much to grant,
   Adopt me of some other family
   By your unquestion'd word, else I shall live
   Like sinful issues that are left in streets
   By their regardless mothers, and no name   185
   Will be found for me.
ARBACES.   I will hear no more.
   [*Aside*] Why should there be such music in a voice

---

170. *having part of*] sharing.
182. *Adopt me of*] have me adopted by.

And sin for me to hear it? All the world
May take delight in this, and 'tis damnation
For me to do so.—You are fair and wise   190
And virtuous, I think, and he is blest
That is so near you as your brother is;
But you are naught to me but a disease,
Continual torment without hope of ease.
Such an ungodly sickness I have got,   195
That he that undertakes my cure must first
O'erthrow divinity, all moral laws,
And leave mankind as unconfin'd as beasts,
Allowing them to do all actions
As freely as they drink when they desire.   200
Let me not hear you speak again; yet so
I shall but languish for the want of that,
The having which would kill me.—No man here
Offer to speak for her, for I consider
As much as you can say.—I will not toil   205
My body and my mind too. Rest thou there;   [*Sits.*]
Here's one within will labor for you both.

PANTHEA.
    I would I were past speaking.

GOBRIUS.   Fear not, madam;
    The king will alter. 'Tis some sudden change,
    And you shall see it end some other way.   210

PANTHEA.
    Pray God it do.

TIGRANES [*Aside*].
    Though she to whom I swore be here, I cannot
    Stifle my passion longer. If my father
    Should rise again, disquieted with this,
    And charge me to forbear, yet it would out.—   215
    Madam, a stranger and a prisoner begs   [*Apart to* Panthea.]
    To be bid welcome.

PANTHEA.   You are welcome, sir,
    I think; but if you be not, 'tis past me
    To make you so, for I am here a stranger
    Greater than you. We know from whence you come,   220
    But I appear a lost thing, and by whom

Is yet uncertain, found here in the court
And only suffer'd to walk up and down
As one not worth the owning.

SPACONIA [*Aside*].   Oh, I fear
Tigranes will be caught; he looks, methinks,   225
As he would change his eyes with her. Some help
There is above for me, I hope.

TIGRANES.

Why do you turn away and weep so fast,
And utter things that misbecome your looks?
Can you want owning?

SPACONIA [*Aside*].   Oh, 'tis certain so.   230

TIGRANES.

Acknowledge yourself mine—

ARBACES.   How now!

TIGRANES.   —And then
See if you want an owner.

ARBACES.   They are talking.

TIGRANES.

Nations shall own you for their queen.

ARBACES.

Tigranes, art not thou my prisoner?

TIGRANES.

I am.

ARBACES.   And who is this?

TIGRANES.   She is your sister.   235

ARBACES.

She is so—

MARDONIUS [*Aside*].   Is she so again? That's well.

ARBACES.

—And how dare you then offer to change
Words with her?

TIGRANES.

Dare do it! Why, you brought me hither, sir,
To that intent.

ARBACES.   Perhaps I told you so.   240
If I had sworn it, had you so much folly

226, 237. *change*] exchange.

To credit it? The least word that she speaks
Is worth a life. Rule your disorder'd tongue,
Or I will temper it.

SPACONIA [*Aside*].   Blest be that breath.

TIGRANES.

Temper my tongue! Such incivilities   245
As these no barbarous people ever knew.
You break the law of nature and of nations.
You talk to me as if I were a prisoner
For theft. My tongue be temper'd? I must speak
If thunder check me, and I will.

ARBACES.   You will?   250

SPACONIA [*Aside*].

Alas, my fortune!

TIGRANES.   Do not fear his frown;
Dear madam, hear me.

ARBACES.

Fear not my frown! But that 'twere base in me
To fight with one I know I can o'ercome
Again thou shouldst be conquer'd by me.   255

MARDONIUS [*Aside*].

He has one ransom with him already; methinks 'twere
good to fight double or quit.

ARBACES.

Away with him to prison.—Now, sir, see
If my frown be regardless.—Why delay you?
Seize him, Bacurius.—You shall know my word   260
Sweeps like a wind, and all it grapples with
Are as the chaff before it.

TIGRANES.   Touch me not!

ARBACES.

Help there!

---

243. *disorder'd*] (1) disorderly, unruly; (2) speaking contrary to
Arbaces' order.

244. *temper*] restore to moderation, curb.

256. *has . . . him*] is subject to the payment of one ransom.

257. *double or quit*] double or nothing; i.e., the ransom is to be
doubled or canceled.

259. *regardless*] unworthy of respect.

TIGRANES.   Away!
1 GENTLEMAN.   It is in vain to struggle.
2 GENTLEMAN.
     You must be forc'd.
BACURIUS.   Sir, you must pardon us;
     We must obey.   [*They seize him.*]
ARBACES.   Why do you dally there?   265
     Drag him away by anything.
BACURIUS.   Come, sir.
TIGRANES.
     Justice, thou ought'st to give me strength enough
     To shake all these off.—This is tyranny,
     Arbaces, subtler than the burning bull's
     Or that fam'd tyrant's bed. Thou might'st as well   270
     Search in the depth of winter through the snow
     For half starv'd people to bring home with thee
     To show 'em fire and send 'em back again
     As use me thus.
ARBACES.   Let him be close, Bacurius.
     Exeunt Tigranes [*led by the two* Gentlemen] *and* Bacurius.
SPACONIA [*Aside*].
     I ne'er rejoic'd at any ill to him   275
     But this imprisonment; what shall become
     Of me forsaken?
GOBRIUS.   You will not let your sister
     Depart thus discontented from you, sir?
ARBACES.
     By no means, Gobrius; I have done her wrong
     And made myself believe much of myself   280
     That is not in me. [*To* Panthea] You did kneel to me
     Whilst I stood stubborn and regardless by

274.1. *Exeunt . . .* Bacurius.] *Q2*
(*Exit . . .*); om. *Q1*.

___

   269. *burning bull's*] Phalaris, tyrant of Agrigentum, is said to have
disposed of his enemies by roasting them in a brazen bull.
   270. *tyrant's bed*] Procrustes' bed. Procrustes was a legendary Attic
highwayman who bound his victims to an iron bed and either stretched
them or chopped off their legs to make them fit.
   274. *close*] confined, secure.
   282. *regardless*] heedless.

And, like a god incensed, gave no ear
To all your prayers. Behold, I kneel to you.
Show a contempt as large as was my own,   285
And I will suffer it; yet at the last
Forgive me.

PANTHEA.   Oh, you wrong me more in this   [*Kneels.*]
Than in your rage you did; you mock me now.

ARBACES.
Never forgive me then, which is the worst
Can happen to me.

PANTHEA.   If you be in earnest,   290
Stand up and give me but a gentle look
And two kind words, and I shall be in heaven.

ARBACES.
Rise you then too.   [*Rises and raises* Panthea.]
               Here I acknowledge thee
My hope, the only jewel of my life,
The best of sisters, dearer than my breath,   295
A happiness as high as I could think;
And when my actions call thee otherwise,
Perdition light upon me.

PANTHEA.   This is better
Than if you had not frown'd. It comes to me
Like mercy at the block, and when I leave   300
To serve you with my life, your curse be with me.

ARBACES.
Then thus do I salute thee—and again   [*Kisses her.*]
To make this knot the stronger. [*Aside*] Paradise
Is there.—It may be you are still in doubt;
This, this third kiss, blots it out. [*Aside*] I wade in sin   305
And foolishly entice myself along.—
Take her away; see her a prisoner
In her own chamber, closely, Gobrius.

PANTHEA.
Alas, sir, why?

ARBACES.   I must not stay the answer—

---

302. *salute*] greet, in this case with a kiss.
308. *closely*] securely.

Do it.

GOBRIUS.   Good sir—

ARBACES.   No more—do it, I say.   310

MARDONIUS [*Aside*].

This is better and better.

PANTHEA.

Yet hear me speak.

ARBACES.   I will not hear you speak.—

Away with her; let no man think to speak

For such a creature, for she is a witch,

A poisoner, and a traitor.   315

GOBRIUS.

Madam, this office grieves me.

PANTHEA.   Nay, 'tis well;

The king is pleas'd with it.

ARBACES.

Bessus, go you along too with her.—I will prove

All this that I have said, if I may live

So long. But I am desperately sick,   320

For she has given me poison in a kiss—

She had it 'twixt her lips—and with her eyes

She witches people. Go without a word.—

                    Exeunt omnes praeter Arbaces, Mardonius.

Why should you that have made me stand in war

Like fate itself, cutting what threads I pleas'd,   325

Decree such an unworthy end of me

And all my glories? What am I, alas,

That you oppose me? If my secret thoughts

Have ever harbor'd swellings against you,

They could not hurt you, and it is in you   330

---

310. S.P. GOBRIUS.] *Q2; Panthea.*   316. GOBRIUS. Madam. . . . PAN-
Q1.   THEA. Nay] *Q2; Q1 assigns as fol-*
                                             lows: Bac. Madam. . . ./ *Gob.* Nay.

323.1. *praeter*] except.

325. *Like . . . pleas'd*] Arbaces' simile is based on the idea common
in European myth that a man's thread of life is spun by one of the
Fates, measured by the second, and cut by the third, the cutting signi-
fying death.

329. *swellings*] feelings of indignation or pride.

To give me sorrow that will render me
Apt to receive your mercy. Rather so—
Let it be rather so—than punish me
With such unmanly sins. Incest is in me
Dwelling already, and it must be holy   335
That pulls it thence.—Where art, Mardonius?

MARDONIUS.
Here, sir.

ARBACES.   I prithee, bear me, if thou canst.
Am I not grown a strange weight?

MARDONIUS.   As you were.

ARBACES.
No heavier?

MARDONIUS.   No, sir.

ARBACES.   Why, my legs
Refuse to bear my body. Oh, Mardonius,   340
Thou hast in field beheld me, when thou know'st
I could have gone, though I could never run.

MARDONIUS.
And so I shall again.

ARBACES.   Oh, no, 'tis past.

MARDONIUS.
Pray ye go; rest yourself.

ARBACES.   Wilt thou hereafter
When they talk of me, as thou shalt hear   345
Nothing but infamy, remember some
Of those things?

MARDONIUS.   Yes, I will.

ARBACES.   I prithee, do;
For thou shalt never see me so again.

MARDONIUS.
I warrant ye.   *Exeunt.*

---

342. *I . . . run*] "To go" often had the sense of "to walk." Hence,
Arbaces means "You have seen me in battle, in circumstances that
would seem more difficult than these. Then I could stand and move
about, although my courage and pride would never have permitted me
to run away." The play is on "gone" (walked/left) and "run" (run/fled).
    349. *I warrant ye*] I promise you (I shall see you so again).

[III.ii]   *Enter* Bessus.

BESSUS.

They talk of fame; I have gotten it in the wars and will
afford any man a reasonable pennyworth. Some will say
they could be content to have it but that it is to be
achieved with danger; but my opinion is otherwise, for if
I might stand still in cannon-proof and have fame fall   5
upon me, I would refuse it. My reputation came princi-
pally by thinking to run away, which nobody knows but
Mardonius, and I think he conceals it to anger me. Before I went to the wars, I came to the town a young
fellow without means or parts to deserve friends; and my   10
empty guts persuaded me to lie and abuse people for my
meat, which I did and they beat me. Then would I fast
two days, till my hunger cried out on me, "Rail still";
then, methought, I had a monstrous stomach to abuse
them again and did it. In this state I continued till they   15
hung me up by th'heels and beat me with hazel sticks,
as if they would have baked me and have cozen'd somebody with me for venison. After this I rail'd and eat
quietly; for the whole kingdom took notice of me for a
baffl'd, whipp'd fellow, and what I said was remember'd   20
in mirth but never in anger, of which I was glad—I would
it were at that pass again. After this, God call'd an aunt
of mine that left two hundred pounds in a cousin's hand
for me, who, taking me to be a gallant young spirit,

---

3. *but*] except.
5. *cannon-proof*] armor that will resist cannon shot.
10. *parts*] abilities, talents.
11–12. *abuse . . . meat*] Bessus, through slander, gained the reputation of a satirical fellow and was invited to dine by those who enjoyed
his remarks about others.
13. *Rail*] complain.
14. *stomach*] (1) inclination, (2) appetite.
16. *hung . . . sticks*] i.e., as one would do the carcass of a deer to
make it tender for cooking. Hanging by the heels, Dyce points out, was
an old punishment for recreant knights.
17. *cozen'd*] deceived.   19. *quietly*] undisturbed.
20. *baffl'd*] disgraced.
22. *pass*] juncture.

rais'd a company for me with the money and sent me   25
into Armenia with 'em. Away I would have run from
them but that I could get no company, and alone I durst
not run. I was never at battle but once, and there I was
running, but Mardonius cudgel'd me; yet I got loose at
last, but was so afraid that I saw no more than my shoul-   30
ders do, but fled with my whole company amongst my
enemies and overthrew 'em. Now the report of my valor
is come over before me, and they say I was a raw young
fellow but now I am improv'd. A plague of their elo-
quence; 'twill cost me many a beating. And Mardonius   35
might help this too if he would; for now they think to
get honor of me, and all the men I have abus'd call me
freshly to account (worthily, as they call it) by the way
of challenge.

Enter a Gentleman.

GENTLEMAN.

Good morrow, Captain Bessus.   40

BESSUS.

Good morrow, sir.

GENTLEMAN.

I come to speak with you—

BESSUS.

You are very welcome.

GENTLEMAN.

—From one that holds himself wronged by you some
three years since. Your worth, he says, is fam'd, and he   45
nothing doubts but you will do him right, as beseems a
soldier.

BESSUS [*Aside*].

A pox on 'em; so they cry all.

GENTLEMAN.

And a slight note I have about me for you, for the delivery of which you must excuse me; it is an office that   50

39.1. *a*] Q2; *om. Q1*.

---

34. *of*] on.
45. *since*] ago.
46. *nothing*] not at all.

friendship calls upon me to do and no way offensive to
you, since I desire but right on both sides. [*Gives him a letter.*]

BESSUS.

'Tis a challenge, sir, is it not?

GENTLEMAN.

'Tis an inviting to the field.

BESSUS.

An inviting! Oh, cry you mercy. [*Aside*] What a compli-   55
ment he delivers it with! He might as agreeably to my
nature present me poison with such a speech. [*Reads
aside*] Um, um, um—reputation; um, um, um—call you
to an account; um, um, um—forc'd to this; um, um, um—
with my sword; um, um, um—like a gentleman; um, um,   60
um—dear to me; um, um, um—satisfaction.—'Tis very
well, sir; I do accept it, but he must await an answer this
thirteen weeks.

GENTLEMAN.

Why, sir, he would be glad to wipe off his stain as soon
as he can.   65

BESSUS.

Sir, upon my credit, I am already engag'd to two hundred and twelve, all which must have their stains wip'd
off, if that be the word, before him.

GENTLEMAN.

Sir, if you be truly engaged but to one, he shall stay a
competent time.   70

BESSUS.

Upon my faith, sir, to two hundred and twelve; and I
have a spent body, too much bruis'd in battle, so that I
cannot fight, I must be plain with you, above three com-
bats a day. All the kindness I can do him is to set him
resolutely in my roll the two hundred and thirteenth   75
man, which is something, for I tell you I think there will
be more after him than before him. I think so. Pray ye
commend me to him and tell him this.

58. Um, um, um . . . um, um, um]   *throughout speech*).
Q2; Um . . . um *Q1* (*and so*   66. S.P. BESSUS.] *Q2; om. Q1.*

70. *competent*] adequate.

GENTLEMAN.

    I will, sir; good morrow to you.

BESSUS.

    Good morrow, good sir. [*Exit* Gentleman.] Certainly my   80
safest way were to print myself a coward, with a discovery
how I came by my credit, and clap it upon every post. I
have received above thirty challenges within this two
hours. Marry, all but the first I put off with engagement,
and, by good fortune, the first is no madder of fighting   85
than I, so that that's reserv'd. The place where it must be
ended is four days' journey off, and our arbitrators are
these: he has chosen a gentleman in travel, and I have a
special friend with a quartan ague likely to hold him this
five year for mine, and when his man comes home, we   90
are to expect my friend's health. If they would send me
challenges thus thick, as long as I liv'd I would have no
other living; I can make seven shillings a day o'th' paper
to the grocers. Yet I learn nothing by all these but a
little skill in comparing of styles. I do find evidently that   95
there is some one scrivener in this town that has a great
hand in writing of challenges, for they are all of a cut
and six of 'em in a hand; and they all end "My reputation is dear to me, and I must require satisfaction."—
Who's there? More paper, I hope. No, 'tis my Lord 100
Bacurius; I fear all is not well betwixt us.

Enter Bacurius.

BACURIUS.

    Now, Captain Bessus, I come about a frivolous matter

---

80. S.D. *Exit* Gentleman.] *Exit:*   88. these] *Q2*; there *Q1*.
Q1; Exit 3. Gen: Q2–8, F (all after   90. five year] *Q2*; time here *Q1*.
l. 79).

---

    81. *print . . . coward*] confess myself a coward in a public notice.
    81. *discovery*] revelation.
    85. *no . . . fighting*] no more inclined to fight.
    86. *reserv'd*] postponed.
    89. *quartan ague*] a fever, with chills recurring every fourth day.
    91. *expect*] await.
    94. *to the grocers*] i.e., by selling it to the grocers for wrapping
paper.
    96. *scrivener*] professional letter-writer, public secretary.
    97. *cut*] style.

caus'd by as idle a report. You know you were a coward.

BACURIUS.

BESSUS.

Very right.

BACURIUS.

And wrong'd me. 105

BESSUS.

True, my lord.

BACURIUS.

But now people will call you valiant—desertlessly, I think; yet, for their satisfaction, I will have you fight with me.

BESSUS.

Oh, my good lord, my deep engagements— 110

BACURIUS.

Tell not me of your engagements, Captain Bessus; it is not to be put off with an excuse. For my own part, I am none of the multitude that believe your conversion from coward.

BESSUS.

My lord, I seek not quarrels, and this belongs not to me; 115 I am not to maintain it.

BACURIUS.

Who then, pray?

BESSUS.

Bessus the coward wrong'd you.

BACURIUS.

Right.

BESSUS.

And shall Bessus the valiant maintain what Bessus the 120 coward did?

BACURIUS.

I prithee, leave these cheating tricks. I swear thou shalt fight with me, or thou shalt be beat extremely and kick'd.

BESSUS.

Since you provoke me thus far, my lord, I will fight with you, and, by my sword, it shall cost me twenty pounds 125 but I will have my leg well a week sooner purposely.

BACURIUS.

Your leg! Why, what ails your leg? I'll do a cure on you;

126. well] Q2; om. Q1.

stand up.

BESSUS.

My lord, this is not noble in you.

BACURIUS.

What dost thou with such a phrase in thy mouth? I will 130
kick thee out of all good words before I leave thee.

[*Kicks him.*]

BESSUS.

My lord, I take this as a punishment for the offense I did
when I was a coward.

BACURIUS.

When thou wert! Confess thyself a coward still, or, by
this light, I'll beat thee into sponge.   135

BESSUS.

Why, I am one.

BACURIUS.

Are you so, sir? And why do you wear a sword then?
Come, unbuckle; quick!

BESSUS.

My lord—

BACURIUS.

Unbuckle, I say, and give it me; or, as I live, thy head 140
will ache extremely.

BESSUS.

It is a pretty hilt, and if your lordship take an affection
to it, with all my heart I present it to you for a new
year's gift.   [*Gives him his sword, with a knife attached.*]

BACURIUS.

I thank you very heartily. Sweet captain, farewell.   145

BESSUS.

One word more. I beseech your lordship to render me my
knife again.

BACURIUS.

Marry, by all means, captain. [*Gives back the knife.*]
Cherish yourself with it, and eat hard, good captain; we
cannot tell whether we shall have any more such. Adieu, 150

143–144. *new year's gift*] Elizabethans customarily exchanged gifts at
New Year's rather than at Christmas.

dear captain.   *Exit.*

BESSUS.

I will make better use of this than of my sword. A base
spirit has this vantage of a brave one: it keeps always at
a stay; nothing brings it down, not beating. I remember
I promis'd the king in a great audience that I would   155
make my backbiters eat my sword to a knife. How to get
another sword I know not, nor know any means left for
me to maintain my credit but impudence; therefore, will
I outswear him and all his followers that this is all is
left uneaten of my sword.   *Exit.*   160

[III.iii]   *Enter* Mardonius.

MARDONIUS.

I'll move the king. He is most strangely alter'd; I guess
the cause, I fear, too right. Heaven has some secret end
in't, and 'tis a scourge, no question, justly laid upon him.
He has followed me through twenty rooms, and ever
when I stay to await his command, he blushes like a girl   5
and looks upon me as if modesty kept in his business; so
turns away from me, but if I go on, he follows me again.
[*Enter* Arbaces.] See, here he is. I do not use this, yet, I
know not how, I cannot choose but weep to see him. His
very enemies, I think, whose wounds have bred his fame,   10
if they should see him now, would find tears in their eyes.

ARBACES [*Aside*].

I cannot utter it. Why should I keep
A breast to harbor thoughts I dare not speak?
Darkness is in my bosom, and there lies
A thousand thoughts that cannot brook the light.   15

[III.iii]   13. thoughts . . . speak?] *Theo-*
8. S.D. *Enter* Arbaces.] *Q2; om.*   *bald*; thoughts? . . . speake:
Q1.   *Q1–8, F.*

153–154. *keeps . . . stay*] remains in a permanent condition.
156. *backbiters*] slanderers.
[III.iii]
1. *move*] prompt (the king to reveal what is troubling him).
8. *do not use*] am not accustomed to.

How wilt thou vex me when this deed is done,
Conscience, that art afraid to let me name it?

MARDONIUS.
How do you, sir?

ARBACES.   Why, very well, Mardonius;
How dost thou do?

MARDONIUS.   Better than you, I fear.

ARBACES.
I hope thou art, for, to be plain with thee,   20
Thou art in hell else. Secret scorching flames,
That far transcend earthly material fires,
Are crept into me, and there is no cure.
Is not that strange, Mardonius, there's no cure?

MARDONIUS.
Sir, either I mistake or there is something hid   25
That you would utter to me.

ARBACES.
So there is, but yet I cannot do it.

MARDONIUS.
Out with it, sir. If it be dangerous, I shall not shrink to
do you service. I shall not esteem my life a weightier
matter than indeed it is. I know 'tis subject to more   30
chances than it hath hours, and I were better lose it in
my king's cause than with an ague, or a fall, or, sleeping,
to a thief, as all these are probable enough. Let me but
know what I shall do for you.

ARBACES [Aside].
It will not out.—Were you with Gobrius,   35
And bade him give my sister all content
The place affords, and give her leave to send
And speak to whom she please?

MARDONIUS.   Yes, sir, I was.

ARBACES.
And did you to Bacurius say as much

19. do] Q2; om. Q1.   32. a fall] Q2; fall Q1.
23. Are] Q2; Art Q1.

32. *ague*] fever.

About Tigranes?

MARDONIUS.   Yes.

ARBACES.   That's all my business.   40

MARDONIUS.

Oh, say not so.
You had an answer of all this before.
Besides, I think this business might be utter'd
More carelessly.

ARBACES.

Come, thou shalt have it out; I do beseech thee,   45
By all the love thou hast profess'd to me,
To see my sister from me.

MARDONIUS.   Well, and what?

ARBACES.

That's all.

MARDONIUS.   That's strange. Shall I say nothing to her?

ARBACES.

Not a word;
But if thou lovest me, find some subtle way   50
To make her understand by signs.

MARDONIUS.   But what?
What should I make her understand?

ARBACES.

Oh, Mardonius, for that I must be pardon'd.

MARDONIUS.

You may, but I can only see her then.

ARBACES.

'Tis true.   55
Bear her this ring then, and, on more advice,
Thou shalt speak to her. Tell her I do love
My kindred all, wilt thou?

MARDONIUS.

Is there no more?

ARBACES.   Oh, yes. And her the best,
Better than any brother loves his sister.   60
That's all.

MARDONIUS.   Methinks this need not have been

---

42. of] to.
56. on more advice] as I have considered the matter more carefully.

Delivered with such a caution; I'll do it.

ARBACES.

There is more yet—wilt thou be faithful to me?

MARDONIUS.

Sir, if I take upon me to deliver it
After I hear it, I'll pass through fire to do it.   65

ARBACES.

I love her better than a brother ought.
Dost thou conceive me?

MARDONIUS.

I hope I do not, sir.

ARBACES.   No? Thou art dull.
Kneel down before her, and ne'er rise again
Till she will love me.

MARDONIUS.   Why, I think she does.   70

ARBACES.

But better than she does—another way—
As wives loves husbands.

MARDONIUS.   Why, I think there are
Few wives that love their husbands better than
She does you.

ARBACES.

Thou wilt not understand me. Is it fit   75
This should be utter'd plainly? Take it, then,
Naked as it is. I would desire her love
Lasciviously, lewdly, incestuously,
To do a sin that needs must damn us both
And thee too. Dost thou understand me now?   80

MARDONIUS.

Yes. There's your ring again. What have I done
Dishonestly in my whole life, name it,
That you should put so base a business to me?

ARBACES.

Didst thou not tell me thou wouldst do it?

MARDONIUS.

Yes, if I undertook it; but if all   85
My hairs were lives, I would not be engag'd

62. a] *Q2; om. Q1.*

In such a cause to save my last life.

ARBACES.

Oh, guilt, how poor and weak a thing art thou!
This man that is my servant, whom my breath
Might blow about the world, might beat me here,   90
Having his cause, whilst I, press'd down with sin,
Could not resist him.—Dear Mardonius,
It was a motion misbeseeming man,
And I am sorry for it.

MARDONIUS.

Pray God you may be so. You must understand, nothing   95
that you can utter can remove my love and service from
my prince. But otherwise, I think I shall not love you
more; for you are sinful, and, if you do this crime, you
ought to have no laws, for after this it will be great injus-
tice in you to punish any offender for any crime. For   100
myself, I find my heart too big; I feel I have not patience
to look on whilst you run these forbidden courses. Means
I have none but your favor, and I am rather glad that I
shall lose 'em both together than keep 'em with such conditions. I shall find a dwelling amongst some people   105
where, though our garments perhaps be coarser, we shall
be richer far within and harbor no such vices in 'em.
God preserve you and mend you.

ARBACES.

Mardonius! Stay, Mardonius! For though
My present state require nothing but knaves   110
To be about me, such as are prepar'd
For every wicked act, yet who does know
But that my loathed fate may turn about
And I have use of honest men again?
I hope I may. I prithee, leave me not.   115

Enter Bessus *to them.*

BESSUS.

Where is the king?

MARDONIUS.

There.

---

93. *motion*] attempt to persuade, instigation.

BESSUS.
    An't please your majesty, there's the knife.

ARBACES.
    What knife?

BESSUS.
    The sword is eaten.   120

MARDONIUS.
    Away, you fool. The king is serious
    And cannot now admit your vanities.

BESSUS.
    Vanities! I am no honest man if my enemies have not
    brought it to this. What, do you think I lie?

ARBACES.
    No, no; 'tis well, Bessus, 'tis very well.   125
    I am glad on't.

MARDONIUS.
    If your enemies brought it to that, your enemies are
    cutlers. Come, leave the king.

BESSUS.
    Why, may not valor approach him?

MARDONIUS.
    Yes, but he has affairs. Depart, or I shall be something 130
    unmannerly with you.

ARBACES.
    No, let him stay, Mardonius, let him stay.
    I have occasions with him very weighty,
    And I can spare you now.

MARDONIUS.
    Sir?   135

ARBACES.
    Why, I can spare you now.

BESSUS.
    Mardonius, give way to the state affairs.

125–127. well./ . . . MARDONIUS. If]   129–131. BESSUS. . . . you.]   Q2;
Q2; well./ Mar. I. . . . If Q1.   om. Q1.

---

   124. brought . . . this] caused this to happen.
   128. cutlers] tradesmen who made, sold, and repaired knives.
   130. something] somewhat.

MARDONIUS.

Indeed, you are fitter for his present purpose. *Exit.*

ARBACES.

Bessus, I should employ thee; wilt thou do't?

BESSUS.

Do't for you? By this air, I will do anything without ex- 140
ception, be it a good, bad, or indifferent thing.

ARBACES.

Do not swear.

BESSUS.

By this light, but I will; anything whatsoever.

ARBACES.

But I shall name a thing
Thy conscience will not suffer thee to do. 145

BESSUS.

I would fain hear that thing.

ARBACES.

Why, I would have thee get my sister for me;
Thou understand'st me—in a wicked manner.

BESSUS.

Oh, you would have a bout with her? I'll do't; I'll do't,
i'faith. 150

ARBACES.

Wilt thou? Dost make no more on't?

BESSUS.

More? No. Why, is there anything else? If there be, tell
me; it shall be done too.

ARBACES.

Hast thou no greater sense of such a sin?
Thou art too wicked for my company, 155
Though I have hell within me, and mayst yet
Corrupt me further. Pray thee, answer me,

140. Do't] *Q2*; Doe *Q1*.   149. a bout] *Q7*; about *Q1–6*.
148. understand'st] *Q2*; under-   153. too] *Q2; om. Q1*.
stands *Q1*.

139. *should*] want to.
145. *suffer*] permit.
146. *fain*] be glad to.

How do I show to thee after this motion?

BESSUS.

Why, your majesty looks as well, in my opinion, as ever
you did since you were born.   160

ARBACES.

But thou appearest to me after thy grant
The ugliest, loathed, detestable thing
That I have ever met with. Thou hast eyes
Like flames of sulphur, which, methinks, do dart
Infection on me, and thou hast a mouth   165
Enough to take me in, where there do stand
Four rows of iron teeth.

BESSUS.

I feel no such thing. But 'tis no matter how I look; I'll do
your business as well as they that look better. And when
this is dispatch'd, if you have a mind to your mother, tell   170
me, and you shall see I'll set it hard.

ARBACES.

My mother!—Heaven forgive me to hear this;
I am inspir'd with horror.—I hate thee
Worse than my sin, which, if I could come by,
Should suffer death eternal, ne'er to rise   175
In any breast again. Know I will die
Languishing mad, as I resolve I shall,
Ere I will deal by such an instrument.
Thou art too sinful to employ in this.
Out of the world; away!   [*Beats him.*]

BESSUS.   What do you mean, sir?   180

ARBACES.

Hung 'round with curses, take thy fearful flight
Into the deserts, where, 'mongst all the monsters,
If thou find'st one so beastly as thyself,
Thou shalt be held as innocent.

BESSUS.   Good sir—

ARBACES.

If there were no such instruments as thou,   185
We kings could never act such wicked deeds.

---

158. *motion*] proposal (cf. 1. 93).
171. *set it hard*] go at it vigorously.

Seek out a man that mocks divinity,
That breaks each precept both of God's and man's
And nature's too and does it without lust
Merely because it is a law and good,   190
And live with him, for him thou canst not spoil.
Away, I say.   *Exit* Bessus.
    I will not do this sin.
I'll press it here till it do break my breast.
It heaves to get out; but thou art a sin,
And, spite of torture, I will keep thee in. [*Exit.*] 195

Finis Actus Tertii.

[IV.i]   *Enter* Gobrius, Panthea, Spaconia.

GOBRIUS.
 Have you written, madam?
PANTHEA.   Yes, good Gobrius.
GOBRIUS.
 And with a kindness and such winning words
 As may provoke him at one instant feel
 His double fault—your wrong and his own rashness?
PANTHEA.
 I have sent words enough, if words may win him 5
 From his displeasure, and such words, I hope,
 As shall gain much upon his goodness, Gobrius.
 Yet fearing, since th'are many and a woman's,
 A poor belief may follow, I have woven
 As many truths within 'em to speak for me, 10
 That, if he be but gracious and receive 'em—
GOBRIUS.
 Good lady, be not fearful. Though he should not
 Give you your present end in this, believe it,
 You shall feel (if your virtue can induce you

192. S.D. *Exit* Bessus.] *after* sin [IV.i]
Q1–8, F.   12. Though] *Q2*; If *Q1*.

189. *lust*] pleasure, desire.
[IV.i]
 2. *kindness*] naturalness.
 13. *present end*] immediate object (i.e., your release).

To labor out this tempest, which I know   15
Is but a poor proof against your patience)
All those contents your spirit will arrive at
Newer and sweeter to you. Your royal brother
(When he shall once collect himself and see
How far he has been asunder from himself,   20
What a mere stranger to his golden temper)
Must from those roots of virtue (never dying,
Though somewhat stopp'd with humor) shoot again
Into a thousand glories, bearing his fair branches
High as our hopes can look at, straight as justice,   25
Loaden with ripe contents. He loves you dearly—
I know it—and I hope I need not further
Win you to understand it.

PANTHEA.   I believe it.
But howsoever, I am sure I love him dearly,
So dearly that if anything I write   30
For my enlarging should beget his anger—
Heaven be a witness with me, and my faith—
I had rather live entomb'd here.

GOBRIUS.

You shall not feel a worse stroke than your grief;
I am sorry 'tis so sharp. I kiss your hand   35
And this night will deliver this true story
With this hand to your brother.

PANTHEA.   Peace go with you;
You are a good man.   *Exit* Gobrius.
                    My Spaconia,
Why are you ever sad thus?

29. But] *Q2; om. Q1.*   38. S.D. *Exit* Gobrius.] *Q2; Exit.*
                                          after brother, *l. 37 Q1.*

---

15. *labor out*] endure; "labor" is a seaman's term, here consistent
with the metaphor, meaning, when used of ships, "roll or pitch heavily"
(*OED, v.* 17).
16. *proof against*] trial of.   17. *contents*] contentments.
19. *collect himself*] get control of himself.
21. *mere*] utter.
23. *humor*] sap, in the context of the metaphor, but with punning
reference to Arbaces' humor or mental disposition.
31. *enlarging*] releasing.

SPACONIA.   Oh, dear lady!

PANTHEA.

    Prithee discover not a way to sadness   40
    Nearer than I have in me. Our two sorrows
    Work like two eager hawks, who shall get highest.
    How shall I lessen thine? For mine, I fear,
    Is easier known than cur'd.

SPACONIA.   Heaven comfort both
    And give yours happy ends, however I   45
    Fall in my stubborn fortunes.

PANTHEA.   This but teaches
    How to be more familiar with our sorrows,
    That are too much our masters. Good Spaconia,
    How shall I do you service?

SPACONIA.   Noblest lady,
    You make me more a slave still to your goodness   50
    And only live to purchase thanks to pay you,
    For that is all the business of my life now.
    I will be bold, since you will have it so,
    To ask a noble favor of you.

PANTHEA.

    Speak it; 'tis yours, for from so sweet a virtue   55
    No ill demand has issue.

SPACONIA.

    Then, ever virtuous, let me beg your will
    In helping me to see the Prince Tigranes,
    With whom I am equal prisoner, if not more.

PANTHEA.

    Reserve me to a greater end, Spaconia;   60
    Bacurius cannot want so much good manners
    As to deny your gentle visitation
    Though you came only with your own command.

SPACONIA.

    I know they will deny me, gracious madam,

59. not] *Q2*; no *Q1*.

---

41. *Nearer*] shorter, more direct.
42. *eager*] hungry (*OED, a.* 7).
50. *still*] continually.
51. *purchase*] obtain.

Being a stranger and so little fam'd,   65
So utter empty of those excellencies
That tame authority. But in you, sweet lady,
All these are natural, beside a power
Deriv'd immediate from your royal brother,
Whose least word in you may command the kingdom.   70

PANTHEA.
More than my word, Spaconia, you shall carry,
For fear it fail you.

SPACONIA.   Dare you trust a token?
Madam, I fear I'm grown too bold a beggar.

PANTHEA.
You are a pretty one, and trust me, lady,
It joys me I shall do a good to you   75
Though to myself I never shall be happy.
Here, take this ring, and from me as a token
Deliver it; I think they will not stay you.
So all your own desires go with you, lady.

SPACONIA.
And sweet peace to your grace.

PANTHEA.   Pray God I find it.   *Exeunt.*   80

[IV.ii]   *Enter* Tigranes.

TIGRANES.
Fool that I am, I have undone myself
And with mine own hand turn'd my fortune 'round,
That was a fair one. I have childishly
Played with my hope so long till I have broke it,
And now too late I mourn for't. Oh, Spaconia,   5
Thou hast found an even way to thy revenge now.
Why didst thou follow me, like a faint shadow,
To wither my desires? But, wretched fool,
Why did I plant thee 'twixt the sun and me

67. tame] *Q2*; have *Q1*.   [IV.ii]
71. word] *Q2*; words *Q1*.   2. turn'd] *Q2*; turne *Q1*.

___

67. *tame*] Cf. II.i.71 and IV.ii.199.
[IV.ii]
    6. *even*] straightforward.

To make me freeze thus? Why did I prefer her   10
To the fair princess?—Oh, thou fool, thou fool,
Thou family of fools, live like a slave still
And in thee bear thine own hell and thy torment;
Thou hast deserv'd it. Couldst thou find no lady
But she that has thy hopes to put her to   15
And hazard all thy peace? None to abuse
But she that lov'd thee ever, poor Spaconia,
And so much lov'd thee that in honesty
And honor thou art bound to meet her virtues?
She that forgot the greatness of her griefs   20
And miseries that must follow such mad passions,
Endless and wild as woman's; she that for thee
And with thee lost her liberty, her name,
And country. You have paid me equal, heavens,
And sent my own rod to correct me with,   25
A woman. For inconstancy I'll suffer;
Lay it on, justice, till my soul melt in me
For my unmanly, beastly, sudden doting
Upon a new face, after all my oaths,
Many and strange ones.   30
I feel my old fire flame again and burn
So strong and violent that should I see her
Again, the grief and that would kill me.

Enter Bacurius *and* Spaconia.

BACURIUS.   Lady,
Your token I acknowledge; you may pass.
There is the king.
SPACONIA.   I thank your lordship for it. *Exit* Bacurius.   35
TIGRANES [*Aside*].
She comes, she comes. Shame hide me ever from her.

24. me equal, heavens] *Q2*; me   33–34. me. . . . Lady,/ Your] *Q2*;
equall Heavens *Q1*.   Ladie./ *Enter Bac. and Spac./*
                                     Bac. Your *Q1*.

---

10. *prefer*] recommend.
12. *slave*] contemptible person.
19. *to meet*] to equal.
24. *equal*] justly.

Would I were buried or so far remov'd
Light might not find me out. I dare not see her.

SPACONIA.

Nay, never hide yourself, for were you hid
Where earth hides all her riches, near her center,   40
My wrongs, without more day, would light me to you.
I must speak ere I die. Were all your greatness
Doubled upon you, y'are a perjur'd man
And only mighty in the wickedness
Of wronging women. Thou art false, false prince;   45
I live to see it. Poor Spaconia lives
To tell thee thou art false, and then no more.
She lives to tell thee thou art more unconstant
Than all ill women ever were together,
Thy faith as firm as raging overflows   50
That no bank can command, and as lasting
As boys' gay bubbles blown in the air and broken.
The wind is fix'd, to thee; and sooner shall
The beaten mariner with his shrill whistle
Calm the loud murmurs of the troubled main   55
And strike it smooth again, than thy soul fall
To have peace in love with any. Thou art all
That all good men must hate, and if thy story
Shall tell succeeding ages what thou wert,
Oh, let it spare me in it, lest true lovers   60
In pity of my wrongs burn thy black legend
And with their curses shake thy sleeping ashes.

TIGRANES.

Oh! Oh!

SPACONIA.

The destinies, I hope, have pointed out
Our ends alike, that thou mayst die for love,   65

64. S.P. SPACONIA.] *Q2; om. Q1.*

---

53. *to*] compared to.
54–56. *beaten . . . again*] Spaconia speaks ironically, as a well-known
seaman's superstition is that whistling raises the wind. This belief was
held in England at least by the early sixteenth century (*OED*, s.v.
"whistle" *v.* 1).
61. *legend*] inscription (on Tigranes' tomb).

Though not for me, for, this assure thyself,
The princess hates thee deadly and will sooner
Be won to marry with a bull, and safer,
Than such a beast as thou art. [*Aside*] I have struck,
I fear, too deep; beshrow me for't.—Sir,   70
This sorrow works me, like a cunning friendship,
Into the same piece with it. [*Aside*] He's asham'd;
Alas, I have been too rugged.—Dear my lord,
I am sorry I have spoken anything,
Indeed I am, that may add more restraint   75
To that too much you have. Good sir, be pleas'd
To think it was a fault of love, not malice,
And do as I will do—forgive it, prince;
I do, and can, forgive the greatest sins
To me you can repent of. Pray believe me.   80

TIGRANES.
Oh, my Spaconia! Oh, thou virtuous woman!

SPACONIA.
No more; the king, sir.

Enter Arbaces, Bacurius, *and* Mardonius.

ARBACES.
Have you been careful of our noble prisoner,
That he want nothing fitting for his greatness?

BACURIUS.
I hope his grace will quit me for my care, sir.   85

ARBACES.
'Tis well.—Royal Tigranes, health.

TIGRANES.
More than the strictness of this place can give, sir,
I offer back again to great Arbaces.

ARBACES.
We thank you, worthy prince, and pray excuse us;
We have not seen you since your being here.   90

---

68. *won*] persuaded.
70. *beshrow*] beshrew, curse (use with weakened force).
71. *works*] (1) weaves, (2) agitates.
85. *quit*] absolve.
87. *strictness*] (1) narrowness (with reference to the physical dimensions of his place of confinement), (2) severity.

I hope your noble usage has been equal
With your own person. Your imprisonment,
If it be any, I dare say is easy
And shall not outlast two days.

TIGRANES.   I thank you.
My usage here has been the same it was,   95
Worthy a royal conqueror. For my restraint,
It came unkindly because much unlook'd for,
But I must bear it.

ARBACES.
What lady is that, Bacurius?

BACURIUS.
One of the princess' women, sir.   100

ARBACES.
I fear'd it. Why comes she hither?

BACURIUS.
To speak with the Prince Tigranes.

ARBACES.
From whom, Bacurius?

BACURIUS.
From the princess, sir.

ARBACES.
I know I had seen her.   105

MARDONIUS [*Aside*].
His fit begins to take him now again; 'tis a strange fever
and 'twill shake us all anon, I fear. Would he were well
cur'd of this raging folly. Give me the wars, where men
are mad and may talk what they list and held the bravest
fellows. This pelting, prattling peace is good for nothing.   110
Drinking's a virtue to it.

ARBACES.
I see there's truth in no man, nor obedience
But for his own ends. Why did you let her in?

BACURIUS.
It was your own command to bar none from him;
Beside, the princess sent her ring, sir, for my warrant.   115

---

97. *unkindly*] unnaturally, unexpectedly.
109. *list*] please.
110. *pelting*] worthless, paltry.

ARBACES.

A token to Tigranes, did she not?
Sirrah, tell truth.

BACURIUS.   I do not use to lie, sir;
'Tis no way I eat or live by. And I think
This is no token, sir.

MARDONIUS [*Aside*].

This combat has undone him. If he had been well beaten,   120
he had been temperate. I shall never see him handsome
again till he have a horseman's staff pok'd through his
shoulders or an arm broke with a bullet.

ARBACES.

I am trifled with.

BACURIUS.

Sir?   125

ARBACES.

I know it, as I know thee to be false.

MARDONIUS [*Aside*].

Now the clap comes.

BACURIUS.

You never knew me so, sir. I dare speak it
And durst a worse man tell me though my better.

MARDONIUS [*Aside*].

'Tis well said, by my soul.   130

ARBACES.

Sirrah, you answer as you had no life.

BACURIUS.

That I fear, sir, to lose nobly.

ARBACES.

I say, sir, once again—

BACURIUS.

You may say, sir, what you please.

---

117. *I . . . use*] I am not accustomed.
121. *handsome*] seemly, easy to deal with.
122. *staff*] spear, lance.
127. *clap*] thunderclap.
129. *durst . . . better*] "Durst" is here used as though it were present
tense (*OED*, s.v. "dare" *v.*¹ 5), the meaning of the phrase being "and
dare a man inferior to me in spirit to tell me I am false though he be
my social superior."

MARDONIUS [*Aside*].

     Would I might do so.

ARBACES.   I will, sir, and say openly   135

     This woman carries letters. By my life,

     I know she carries letters—this woman does it.

MARDONIUS.

     Would Bessus were here to take her aside and search her;

     he would quickly tell you what she carried, sir.

ARBACES.

     I have found it out; this woman carries letters.   140

MARDONIUS [*Aside*].

     If this hold, 'twill be an ill world for bawds, chamber-

     maids, and post-boys. I thank God I have none but his

     letters-patents, things of his own inditing.

ARBACES.

     Prince, this cunning cannot do it.

TIGRANES.

     Do what, sir? I reach you not.   145

ARBACES.

     It shall not serve your turn, prince.

TIGRANES.

     Serve my turn, sir?

ARBACES.

     Ay, sir, it shall not serve your turn.

TIGRANES.

     Be plainer, good sir.

ARBACES.

     This woman shall carry no more letters back to your love,   150

     Panthea. By heaven, she shall not; I say she shall not.

MARDONIUS [*Aside*].

     This would make a saint swear like a soldier and a soldier

     like Termagant.

145. Do] *Q2; om. Q1.*

---

     141. *hold*] continue.
     143. *letters-patents*] official documents, credentials.
     143. *inditing*] composition.
     145. *reach you not*] do not understand you.
     153. *Termagant*] a blustering Saracen diety who often appeared in medieval drama and romance.

TIGRANES.
This beats me more, king, than the blows you gave me.
ARBACES.
Take 'em away both and together let 'em be prisoners 155
strictly and closely kept, or, sirrah, your life shall answer
it; and let nobody speak with 'em hereafter.
BACURIUS.
Well, I am subject to you and must endure these passions.
SPACONIA [*Aside*].
This is the imprisonment I have look'd for always
And the dear place I would choose.   160
                    Exit Bacurius *with* Tigranes *and* Spaconia.
MARDONIUS.
Sir, have you done well now?
ARBACES.
Dare you reprove it?
MARDONIUS.   No.
ARBACES.   You must be crossing me.
MARDONIUS.
I have no letters, sir, to anger you
But a dry sonnet of my corporal's
To an old saddler's wife, and that I'll burn, sir.   165
'Tis like to prove a fine age for the ignorant.
ARBACES.
How darest thou so often forfeit thy life?
Thou knowest 'tis in my power to take it.
MARDONIUS.
Yes, and I know you wonnot, or, if you do,
You'll miss it quickly.   170
ARBACES.
Why?
MARDONIUS.
Who shall then tell you of these childish follies
When I am dead? Who shall put to his power
To draw those virtues out of a flood of humors
Where they are drown'd and make 'em shine again?   175

---

164. *dry*] unornamented (in the literary sense), matter-of-fact.
173. *put to*] apply.
174. *humors*] passions.

No, cut my head off. Do, kill me.
Then you may talk, and be believ'd, and grow,
And have your too self-glorious temper rock'd
Into a dead sleep and the kingdom with you
Till foreign swords be in your throats and slaughter   180
Be everywhere about you, like your flatterers.
Do, kill me.

ARBACES.
Prithee, be tamer, good Mardonius.
Thou know'st I love thee; nay, I honor thee.
Believe it, good old soldier, I am all thine,   185
But I am rack'd clean from myself. Bear with me;
Wo't thou bear with me, my Mardonius?

Enter Gobrius.

MARDONIUS.
There comes a good man. Love him too; he's temperate.
You may live to have need of such a virtue;
Rage is not still in fashion.

ARBACES.   Welcome, good Gobrius.   190

GOBRIUS.
My service and this letter to your grace.

ARBACES.
From whom?

GOBRIUS.
From the rich mine of virtue and all beauty,
Your mournful sister.

ARBACES.
She is in prison, Gobrius, is she not?   195

GOBRIUS.
She is, sir, till your pleasure do enlarge her,

178. rock'd] *Theobald*; rott *Q1–8,F.*   187. my] *Q2*; good *Q1.*
180. Till] *Q2*; Like *Q1.*

---

186. *rack'd*] painfully drawn, with reference to the instrument of
torture which pulled apart the joints of the unfortunate person
strapped to it.
187. *my*] Q1's *good* is probably a memorial error induced by *good*
in l. 183.
190. *still*] always.
196. *enlarge*] release.

Which on my knees I beg. Oh, 'tis not fit
That all the sweetness of the world in one,
The youth and virtue that would tame wild tigers
And wilder people that have known no manners,   200
Should live thus cloister'd up. For your love's sake,
If there be any in that noble heart
To her, a wretched lady and forlorn,
Or for her love to you, which is as much
As nature and obedience ever gave,   205
Have pity on her beauties.

ARBACES.

Prithee stand up. 'Tis true she is too fair
And all these commendations but her own.
Would thou hadst never so commended her,
Or I ne'er liv'd to have heard it, Gobrius.   210
If thou but knew of the wrong her beauty does her,
Thou wouldst in pity of her be a liar.
Thy ignorance has drawn me, wretched man,
Whither myself nor thou canst well tell. Oh, my fate,
I think she loves me, but I fear another   215
Is deeper in her heart. How think'st thou, Gobrius?

GOBRIUS.

I do beseech your grace, believe it not,
For let me perish if it be not false.
Good sir, read her letter.

MARDONIUS [*Aside*].

This love, or what a devil is it, I know not, begets more 220
mischief than a wake. I had rather be well beaten, starv'd,
or lousy than live within the air on't. He that had seen
this brave fellow charge through a grove of pikes but
t'other day, and look upon him now, will ne'er believe
his eyes again. If he continue thus but two days more, a   225
tailor may beat him with one hand tied behind him.

199. tame] *Q2*; have *Q1*.

---

199. *tame*] Cf. II.i.71 and IV.i.67.
221. *wake*] see I.i.218.
222. *on't*] of it.
226. *tailor*] Apparently quite early the proverb "It takes nine [or two or three] tailors [i.e., tellers, strokes on the death bell] to make a

ARBACES.

    Alas, she would be at liberty,
    And there be thousand reasons, Gobrius,
    Thousands that will deny it,
    Which if she knew, she would contentedly   230
    Be where she is and bless her virtue for it
    And me, though she were closer—she would, Gobrius;
    Good man, indeed she would.

GOBRIUS.   Then, good sir, for
    Her satisfaction send for her and with
    Reason make her know why she must live   235
    Thus from you.

ARBACES.   I will; go bring her to me.   *Exeunt.*

[IV.iii]   *Enter* Bessus, *and two* Swordmen, *and a* Boy.

BESSUS.

    Y'are very welcome both.—Some stools there, boy,
    And reach a table.—Gentlemen o'th' sword,
    Pray sit without more compliment.—Begone, child.

                        [Boy *withdraws.*]

    I have been curious in the searching of you,
    Because I understood you wise and valiant persons.   5

1 SWORDMAN.

    We understand ourselves, sir.

BESSUS.

    Nay, gentlemen and my dear friends o'th' sword,
    No compliment, I pray; but to the cause
    I hang upon, which, in few, is my honor.

229. Thousands] *Q2; om. Q1.*

---

man" was wrongly understood to refer to the fashioner of clothes, and
the tailor became the proverbial type of the inadequate man. Cf. Feeble
in *2 Henry IV* and the listings of M. P. Tilley, *A Dictionary of the
Proverbs in England* . . . (1950), T23.

    232. *closer*] confined more closely.

[IV.iii]

    0.1. *Swordmen*] fighting men armed with the sword, but sometimes,
as here, used pejoratively, implying a bully, a swaggerer.

    4. *curious*] careful.

    9. *hang upon*] am undecided about.

    9. *in few*] in a few words.

2 SWORDMAN.

    You cannot hang too much, sir, for your honor.   10

    But to your cause—be wise and speak truth.

BESSUS.

    My first doubt is my beating by my prince.

1 SWORDMAN.

    Stay there a little, sir. Do you doubt a beating,

    Or have you had a beating by your prince?

BESSUS.

    Gentleman o'th' sword, my prince has beaten me.   15

2 SWORDMAN.

    Brother, what think you of this case?

1 SWORDMAN.

    If he have beaten him, the case is clear.

2 SWORDMAN.

    If he have beaten him, I grant the case.

    But how? We cannot be too subtle in this business.

    I say, but how?

BESSUS.   Even with his royal hand.   20

1 SWORDMAN.

    Was it a blow of love or indignation?

BESSUS.

    'Twas twenty blows of indignation, gentlemen,

    Besides two blows o'th' face.

2 SWORDMAN.

    Those blows o'th' face have made a new case on't;

    The rest were but an honorable rudeness.   25

1 SWORDMAN.

    Two blows o'th' face and given by a worse man,

    I must confess, as we swordmen say, had turn'd

    The business. Mark me, brother—by a worse man.

    But being by his prince, had they been ten

    And those ten drawn ten teeth beside the hazard   30

    Of his nose forever—all these had been but favors.

---

12. *doubt*] uncertainty, but the First Swordman shifts the meaning to "fear" (l. 13).

19, 20. *how*] why, for what reason, but Bessus understands the word to mean "in what manner" (l. 20).

24. *on't*] of it.

27–28. *turn'd the business*] been decisive, finished the matter.

This is my flat opinion, which I'll die in.

2 SWORDMAN.

The king may do much, captain, believe it,
For had he crack'd your skull through like a bottle
Or broke a rib or two with crossing of you,   35
Yet you had lost no honor. This is strange,
You may imagine, but this is truth now, captain.

BESSUS.

I will be glad to embrace it, gentlemen.
But how far may he strike me?

1 SWORDMAN.   There's another,
A new cause rising from the time and distance,   40
In which I will deliver my opinion.
He may strike, beat, or cause to be beaten,
For these are natural to man. Your prince,
I say, may beat you so far forth as his
Dominion reacheth—that's for the distance.   45
The time—ten mile a day, I take it.

2 SWORDMAN.

Brother, you err; 'tis fifteen mile a day.
His stage is ten; his beatings are fifteen.

BESSUS.

'Tis o'the longest, but we subjects must—

1 SWORDMAN.

—Be subject to it. You are wise and virtuous.   50

BESSUS.

Obedience ever makes that noble use on't,
To which I dedicate my beaten body.
I must trouble you a little further, gentlemen o'th' sword.

38. gentlemen] Q2; gentleman Q1.   ous./ 1. Obedience . . . ont,/ To
49–53. BESSUS. 'Tis . . . sword.] Q2;   bodie;/ I . . . sword. Q1.
Bes. Tis . . . must/ Be . . . vertu-

---

32. *flat*] positive.
35. *crossing*] thwarting, opposing, possibly with "making angry" as
a subsidiary meaning. The Second Swordman is, of course, speaking
euphemistically.
39. *how far*] to what degree, how much, but the First Swordman
understands Bessus to mean "for what distance."
48. *stage*] a division of a road (or, more generally, a journey) at the
end of which fresh horses could be obtained.

2 SWORDMAN.

> No trouble at all to us, sir, if we may
> Profit your understanding; we are bound   55
> By virtue of our calling to utter
> Our opinions shortly and discreetly.

BESSUS.

> My sorest business is I have been kick'd.

2 SWORDMAN.

> How far, sir?

BESSUS.

> Not to flatter myself in it, all over—   60
> My sword lost but not forc'd, for discreetly
> I render'd it to save that imputation.

1 SWORDMAN.

> It showed discretion, the best part of valor.

2 SWORDMAN.

> Brother, this is a pretty case; pray ponder on't.
> Our friend here has been kick'd.

1 SWORDMAN.   He has so, brother.   65

2 SWORDMAN.

> Sorely, he says. Now had he sit down here
> Upon the mere kick, it had been cowardly.

1 SWORDMAN.

> I think it had been cowardly indeed.

2 SWORDMAN.

> But our friend has redeem'd it in delivering
> His sword without compulsion, and that man   70
> That took it of him I pronounce a weak one
> And his kicks nullities.
> He should have kick'd him after the delivery,
> Which is the confirmation of a coward.

1 SWORDMAN.

> Brother, I take it you mistake the question.   75

61. lost . . . forc'd] *Theobald;*
forst . . . lost *Q1–8, F.*

---

58. *sorest*] (1) most pressing, (2) most painful.
59. *how far?*] for what distance? But Bessus understands "to what extent" (l. 60).
64. *pretty*] complex, requiring ingenuity for solution.

For say that I were kick'd—

2 SWORDMAN.   I must not say so,
Nor I must not hear it spoke by th' tongue of man.
You kick'd, dear brother! You are merry.

1 SWORDMAN.
But put the case I were kick'd.

2 SWORDMAN.   Let them put it
That are things weary of their lives and know   80
Not honor. Put the case you were kick'd!

1 SWORDMAN.
I do not say I was kick'd.

2 SWORDMAN.   —Nor no silly
Creature that wears his head without a case,
His soul in a skin coat. You kick'd, dear brother!

BESSUS.
Nay, gentlemen, let us do what we shall do   85
Truly and honestly.—Good sir, to th' question.

1 SWORDMAN.
Why then, I say, suppose your boy kick'd, captain.

2 SWORDMAN.
The boy may be suppos'd; he's liable.
But kick my brother?

1 SWORDMAN [To Bessus].
A foolish, forward zeal, sir, in my friend.—   90
But to the boy; suppose the boy were kick'd.

BESSUS.
I do suppose it.

1 SWORDMAN.   Has your boy a sword?

BESSUS.
Surely, no; I pray suppose a sword too.

1 SWORDMAN.
I do suppose it. You grant your boy was kick'd, then?

81. the] Q2; om. Q1.

---

79. *put the case*] suppose.
83. *without a case*] (1) unhelmeted, (2) possibly, without a spare.
The *OED* (*sb.*² 8.b) conjecturally cites *The Maid in the Mill*, II.ii, in
support of the latter meaning, but it occurs elsewhere, e.g., *The White
Devil*, ed. John Russell Brown (1960), V.vi.20.
88. *liable*] (1) suitable, (2) in the legal sense, subject (to kicking).

2 SWORDMAN.

    By no means, captain; let it be suppos'd still.   95

    This word "grant" makes not for us.

1 SWORDMAN.

    I say this must be granted.

2 SWORDMAN.

    This must be granted, brother?

1 SWORDMAN.

    Ay, this must be granted.

2 SWORDMAN.   Still the "must."

1 SWORDMAN.

    I say this must be granted.   100

2 SWORDMAN.

    Give me the "must" again! Again! Brother, you palter.

1 SWORDMAN.

    I will not hear you, wasp.

2 SWORDMAN.

    Brother,

    I say you palter. The "must" three times together!

    I wear as sharp steel as another man,   105

    And my fox bites as deep. "Musted," my dear brother!

    But to the cause again.

BESSUS.   Nay, look you, gentlemen—

2 SWORDMAN.

    In a word, I ha' done.

1 SWORDMAN [*To* Bessus].

    A tall man but untemperate; 'tis great pity.—

    Once more, suppose the boy kick'd—   110

2 SWORDMAN.

    Forward.

1 SWORDMAN.

    —And, being thoroughly kick'd, laughs at the kicker.

2 SWORDMAN.

    So much for us; proceed.

---

106. "Musted"] *Q2*; musled *Q1*.   112. kicker] *Q2*; kicke *Q1*.

---

101. *palter*] shift your ground, mumble, deal dishonestly.

106. *fox*] sword.

109. *tall*] valiant.

1 SWORDMAN.

> And in this beaten scorn, as I may call it,
> Delivers up his weapon. Where lies the error?   115

BESSUS.

> It lies i'th' beating, sir; I found it
> Four days since.

2 SWORDMAN.

> The error, and a sore one, as I take it,
> Lies in the thing kicking.

BESSUS.

> I understand that well; 'tis sore indeed, sir.   120

1 SWORDMAN.

> That is, according to the man that did it.

2 SWORDMAN.

> There springs a new branch. Whose was the foot?

BESSUS.   A lord's.

1 SWORDMAN.

> The cause is mighty; but had it been two lords
> And both had kick'd you, if you laugh'd, 'tis clear.

BESSUS.

> I did laugh, but how will that help me, gentlemen?   125

2 SWORDMAN.

> Yes, it shall help you, if you laugh'd aloud.

BESSUS.

> As loud as a kick'd man could laugh, I laugh'd, sir.

1 SWORDMAN.

> My reason now: the valiant man is known
> By suffering and contemning. You have
> Enough of both, and you are valiant.   130

2 SWORDMAN.

> If he be sure he has been kick'd enough.
> For that brave sufferance you speak of, brother,
> Consists not in a beating and away
> But in a cudgel'd body from eighteen
> To eight and thirty, in a head rebuk'd   135
> With pots of all size, daggers, stools, and bedstaves.

122. foot] *Q2*; foole *Q1*.   126. S.P. 2 SWORDMAN.] *Q2*; 1. *Q1*.
122. A] *Q2*; Ah *Q1*.

---

129. *contemning*] scorning.

This shows a valiant man.

BESSUS.

 Then I am valiant, as valiant as the proudest,
 For these are all familiar things to me,
 Familiar as my sleep or want of money.   140
 All my whole body's but one bruise with beating;
 I think I have been cudgel'd with all nations
 And almost all religions.

2 SWORDMAN.

 Embrace him, brother; this man is valiant;
 I know it by myself, he's valiant.   145

1 SWORDMAN.

 Captain, thou art a valiant gentleman;
 To abide upon't, a very valiant man.

BESSUS.

 My equal friends o'th' sword, I must request
 Your hands to this.

2 SWORDMAN.   'Tis fit it should be.

BESSUS.

 Boy, get some wine and pen and ink within. [*Exit* Boy.] 150
 Am I clear, gentlemen?

1 SWORDMAN.

 Sir, when the world has taken notice what
 We have done, make much of your body, for,
 I'll pawn my steel, men will be coyer of
 Their legs hereafter.

BESSUS.   I must request you go   155
 Along and testify to the Lord Bacurius,
 Whose foot has struck me, how you find my cause.

2 SWORDMAN.

 We will and tell that lord he must be rul'd,
 Or there be those abroad will rule his lordship. *Exeunt.*

[IV.iv]

 Enter Arbaces *at one door,* Gobrius *and* Panthea *at another.*

---

147. *To abide upon't*] to stand firm on the matter.
148. *equal*] fair, just.
149. *hands*] signatures.

GOBRIUS.
    Sir, here's the princess.

ARBACES.   Leave us then alone.
    For the main cause of her imprisonment
    Must not be heard by any but herself.—   *Exit* Gobrius.
    You are welcome, sister, and I would to God
    I could so bid you by another name.—   5
    [*Aside*] If you above love not such sins as these,
    Circle my heart with thoughts as cold as snow
    To quench these rising flames that harbor here.

PANTHEA.
    Sir, does it please you I should speak?

ARBACES.   Please me?
    Ay, more than all the art of music can,   10
    Thy speech does please me, for it ever sounds
    As thou brought'st joyful, unexpected news.
    And yet it is not fit thou shouldst be heard;
    I prithee, think so.

PANTHEA.   Be it so; I will.
    I am the first that ever had a wrong   15
    So far from being fit to have redress
    That 'twas unfit to hear it; I will back
    To prison rather than disquiet you
    And wait till it be fit.

ARBACES.   No, do not go,
    For I will hear thee with a serious thought.   20
    I have collected all that's man about me
    Together strongly, and I am resolv'd
    To hear thee largely, but, I do beseech thee,
    Do not come nearer to me, for there is
    Something in that that will undo us both.   25

PANTHEA.
    Alas, sir, am I venom?

ARBACES.   Yes, to me.
    Though of thyself I think thee to be in
    As equal a degree of heat or cold
    As nature can make, yet as unsound men

---

3. S.D. *Exit* Gobrius.] *Q2; om. Q1.*   12. brought'st] *Q2;* broughts *Q1.*

23. *largely*] at length.

Convert the sweetest and the nourishing'st meats   30
Into diseases, so shall I, distemper'd,
Do thee. I prithee, draw no nearer to me.

PANTHEA.

Sir, this is that I would: I am of late
Shut from the world, and why it should be thus
Is all I wish to know.

ARBACES.   Why, credit me,   35
Panthea, credit me that am thy brother,
Thy loving brother, that there is a cause
Sufficient, yet unfit for thee to know,
That might undo thee everlastingly
Only to hear. Wilt thou but credit this?   40
By heaven, 'tis true; believe it if thou canst.

PANTHEA.

Children and fools are ever credulous,
And I am both, I think, for I believe.
If you dissemble, be it on your head.
I'll back unto my prison; yet, methinks,   45
I might be kept in some place where you are,
For in myself I find—I know not what
To call it, but it is a great desire
To see you often.

ARBACES.

Fie, you come in a step; what do you mean,   50
Dear sister? Do not so. Alas, Panthea,
Where I am would you be? Why, that's the cause
You are imprison'd, that you may not be
Where I am.

PANTHEA.   Then I must endure it, sir;
God keep you.   55

ARBACES.

Nay, you shall hear the cause in short, Panthea,
And when thou hear'st it, thou wilt blush for me
And hang thy head down like a violet
Full of the morning's dew. There is a way

---

31. *distemper'd*] (1) diseased, (2) out of good temper, disturbed.
33. *that I would*] what I want.
50. *come in*] approach.

To gain thy freedom, but 'tis such a one   60
As puts thee in worse bondage, and I know
Thou wouldst encounter fire and make a proof
Whether the gods have care of innocents
Rather than follow it. Know I have lost
The only difference betwixt man and beast,   65
My reason.

PANTHEA.   Heaven forbid!

ARBACES.   Nay, it is gone,
And I am left as far without a bound
As the wild ocean that obeys the winds;
Each sudden passion throws me as it lists
And overwhelms all that oppose my will.   70
I have beheld thee with a lustful eye.
My heart is set on wickedness, to act
Such sins with thee as I have been afraid
To think of. If thou dar'st consent to this
(Which, I beseech thee, do not), thou mayst gain   75
Thy liberty and yield me a content.
If not, thy dwelling must be dark and close
Where I may never see thee, for God knows,
That laid this punishment upon my pride,
Thy sight at some time will enforce my madness   80
To make a start e'en to thy ravishing.
Now spit upon me and call all reproaches
Thou canst devise together, and at once
Hurl 'em against me, for I am a sickness
As killing as the plague ready to seize thee.   85

PANTHEA.
Far be it from me to revile the king.
But it is true that I should rather choose
To search out death, that else would search out me,
And in a grave sleep with my innocence
Than welcome such a sin. It is my fate;   90
To these cross accidents I was ordain'd

81. e'en] *Q2*; eye *Q1*.

---

69. *lists*] pleases.
81. *make a start*] move suddenly.

And must have patience, and, but that my eyes
Have more of woman in 'em than my heart,
I would not weep. Peace enter you again.

ARBACES.

Farewell, and, good Panthea, pray for me—   95
Thy prayers are pure—that I may find a death,
However soon, before my passions grow
That they forget what I desire is sin,
For thither they are tending. If that happen,
Then I shall force thee, though thou wert a virgin   100
By vow to heaven, and shall pull a heap
Of strange, yet-uninvented sins upon me.

PANTHEA.

Sir, I will pray for you, yet you shall know
It is a sullen fate that governs us.
For I could wish as heartily as you   105
I were no sister to you; I should then
Embrace your lawful love sooner than health.

ARBACES.

Couldst thou affect me then?

PANTHEA.   So perfectly
That, as it is, I ne'er shall sway my heart
To like another.

ARBACES.   Then I curse my birth.   110
Must this be added to my miseries,
That thou art willing too? Is there no stop
To our full happiness but these mere sounds,
"Brother" and "sister"?

PANTHEA.   There is nothing else,
But these, alas, will separate us more   115
Than twenty worlds betwixt us.

ARBACES.   I have liv'd
To conquer men and now am overthrown
Only by words—"brother" and "sister." Where
Have those words dwelling? I will find 'em out
And utterly destroy them, but they are   120

112. stop] *Q2*; steppe *Q1*.

102. *strange*] uncommon, rare.

Not to be grasp'd. Let 'em be men or beasts,
And I will cut 'em from the earth, or towns
And I will raze 'em and then blow 'em up.
Let 'em be seas, and I will drink them off
And yet have unquench'd fire left in my breast. 125
Let 'em be anything but merely voice.

PANTHEA.

But 'tis not in the power of any force
Or policy to conquer them.

ARBACES.   Panthea,
What shall we do? Shall we stand firmly here
And gaze our eyes out?

PANTHEA.   Would I could do so, 130
But I shall weep out mine.

ARBACES.   Accursed man,
Thou bought'st thy reason at too dear a rate,
For thou hast all thy actions bounded in
With curious rules when every beast is free.
What is there that acknowledges a kindred 135
But wretched man? Whoever saw the bull
Fearfully leave the heifer that he lik'd
Because they had one dam?

PANTHEA.   Sir, I disturb you
And myself too; 'twere better I were gone.
I will not be so foolish as I was. 140

ARBACES.

Stay, we will love just as becomes our births,
No otherwise. Brothers and sisters may
Walk hand in hand together; so will we.
Come nearer. Is there any hurt in this?

PANTHEA.

I hope not.

ARBACES.   Faith, there's none at all. 145
And tell me truly now, is there not one
You love above me?

143–144. we./ Come] Q2 (we;/
Come); we/ Come Q1.

128. *policy*] stratagem.
134. *curious*] elaborate.

PANTHEA.   No, by heaven.

ARBACES.   Why yet,
    You sent unto Tigranes, sister.

PANTHEA.   True,
    But for another. For the truth—

ARBACES.   No more;
    I'll credit thee. I know thou canst not lie;   150
    Thou art all truth.

PANTHEA.   But is there nothing else
    That we may do but only walk? Methinks
    Brothers and sisters lawfully may kiss.

ARBACES.
    And so they may, Panthea; so will we
    And kiss again too. We were scrupulous   155
    And foolish, but we will be so no more.   [*They kiss.*]

PANTHEA.
    If you have any mercy, let me go
    To prison, to my death, to anything.
    I feel a sin growing upon my blood
    Worse than all these, hotter, I fear, than yours.   160

ARBACES.
    That is impossible. What should we do?

PANTHEA.
    Fly, sir, for God's sake.

ARBACES.   So we must; away.
    Sin grows upon us more by this delay.   *Exeunt.*

Finis Actus Quarti.

[V.i]   *Enter* Mardonius *and* Ligones.

MARDONIUS.
    Sir, the king has seen your commission and believes it,
    And freely by this warrant gives you leave
    To visit Prince Tigranes, your noble master.

LIGONES.
    I thank his grace and kiss his hands.

MARDONIUS.   But is
    The main of all your business ended in this?   5

147. Why] *Q2; om. Q1.*   163. S.D. *Exeunt.*] *Q2; om. Q1.*

LIGONES.

    I have another, but a worse. I am asham'd.

    It is a business—

MARDONIUS.   You serve a worthy person,

    And a stranger I am sure you are; you may employ me,

    If you please, without your purse. Such offices

    Should ever be their own rewards.   10

LIGONES.

    I am bound to your nobleness.

MARDONIUS.

    I may have need of you, and then this courtesy,

    If it be any, is not ill bestowed.

    But may I civilly desire the rest?

    I shall not be a hurter, if no helper.   15

LIGONES.

    Sir, you shall know I have lost a foolish daughter

    And with her all my patience, pilfer'd away

    By a mean captain of your king's.

MARDONIUS.   Stay there, sir.

    If he have reach'd the noble worth of captain,

    He may well claim a worthy gentlewoman,   20

    Though she were yours and noble.

LIGONES.

    I grant all that too. But this wretched fellow

    Reaches no further than the empty name

    That serves to feed him; were he valiant

    Or had but in him any noble nature   25

    That might hereafter promise him a good man,

    My cares were something lighter and my grave

    A span yet from me.

MARDONIUS.   I confess such fellows

    Be in all royal camps, and have and must be,

    To make the sin of coward more detested   30

    In the mean soldier, that with such a foil

    Sets off much valor. By the description

    I should now guess him to you. It was Bessus;

    I dare almost with confidence pronounce it.

9. offices] *Q2*; Officers *Q1*.

---

27. *something*] somewhat.

LIGONES.

    'Tis such a scurvy name as Bessus; and now   35
    I think, 'tis he.

MARDONIUS.   "Captain" do you call him?

    Believe me, sir, you have a misery
    Too mighty for your age. A pox upon him,
    For that must be the end of all his service.
    Your daughter was not mad, sir?

LIGONES.   No, would she had been; 40
    The fault had had more credit. I would do something.

MARDONIUS.

    I would fain counsel you, but to what I know not.
    He's so below a beating that the women
    Find him not worthy of their distaves and
    To hang him were to cast away a rope;   45
    He's such an airy, thin, unbodied coward
    That no revenge can catch him.
    I'll tell you, sir, and tell you truth; this rascal
    Fears neither God nor man, h'as been so beaten.
    Sufferance has made him wainscot. He has had   50
    Since he was first a slave
    At least three hundred daggers set in his head,
    As little boys do new knives in hot meat.
    There's not a rib in's body, o' my conscience,
    That has not been thrice broken with dry beating, 55
    And now his sides look like to wicker targets,
    Every way bended.
    Children will shortly take him for a wall
    And set their stone-bows in his forehead. He

59. He] *Q2; om. Q1.*

---

42. *would fain*] desire to.

44. *distaves*] short wooden poles on which wool was wound before it
was reeled off to be twisted into thread.

50. *wainscot*] a tough, imported oak used in England for furniture
and panelwork.

51. *was . . . slave*] i.e., did his first contemptible act.

55. *dry beating*] beating that draws no blood.

56. *targets*] shields.

58–61. *Children . . . him*] The sense of this rather strained and
possibly corrupt passage is none too clear. The general idea seems to be

Is of so low a sense, I cannot in   60
A week imagine what should be done to him.

LIGONES.

Sure I have committed some great sin,
That this strange fellow should be made my rod.
I would see him, but I shall have no patience.

MARDONIUS.

'Tis no great matter if you have not. If a laming of him,   65
or such a toy, may do you pleasure, sir, he has it for you,
and I'll help you to him. 'Tis no news to him to have a
leg broke or a shoulder out with being turn'd o'th' stones
like a tansy. Draw not your sword, if you love it, for, of
my conscience, his head will break it. We use him i'th'   70
wars like a ram to shake a wall withal. Here comes the
very person of him; do as you shall find your temper. I
must leave you, but if you do not break him like a bis-
cuit, you are much to blame, sir.   *Exit.*

Enter Bessus *and* Swordmen.

LIGONES.

Is your name Bessus?   75

BESSUS.

Men call me Captain Bessus.

---

74. S.D. *Exit.*] *Ex. Mardo. Q1–8, F.*

---

that Bessus is of so low a sense (understanding, apprehension, or, more
generally, mind) that children, mistaking him for a wall, will discharge
their stone-bows (crossbows which shoot stones) at his forehead. "Set"
could mean "aim, direct" (cf. *OED, v.* 20.c), but "in" as a preposition
did not ordinarily have the meaning of "at" or "toward." Bond believes
that "every way bended" (l. 57) suggests a "comparison to a rough-built
wall, whose jutting stones presents the same variety of surface" as the
wicker targets. He understands "in" as "on" and notes that the stone-
bows "might be leant on a low wall-top to steady their aim." The idea
thus expressed seems unsatisfactory, however, because Bessus, in terms
of the metaphor, should be receiving some sort of punishment, not
aiding in its delivery.

66. *toy*] trifle.
68. *stones*] hearthstones.
69. *tansy*] a cake flavored with tansy, an herb.
69. *of*] on.

LIGONES.

> Then, Captain Bessus, you are a rank rascal, without
> more exordiums, a dirty, frozen slave; and, with the favor
> of your friends here, I will beat you.

2 SWORDMAN.

> Pray use your pleasure, sir; you seem to be   80
> A gentleman.

LIGONES.   Thus, Captain Bessus, thus;   [Beats him.]

> Thus twinge your nose, thus kick you, and thus tread you.

BESSUS.

> I do beseech you, yield your cause, sir, quickly.

LIGONES.

> Indeed, I should have told you that first.

BESSUS.

> I take it so.   85

1 SWORDMAN.

> Captain, 'a should indeed; he is mistaken.

LIGONES.

> Sir, you shall have it quickly and more beating.
> You have stol'n away a lady, Captain Coward,
> And such a one—   [Beats him again.]

BESSUS.   Hold! I beseech you, hold, sir!

> I never yet stole any living thing   90
> That had a tooth about it.

LIGONES.

> Sir, I know you dare lie—

BESSUS.

> —With none but summer whores, upon my life, sir.
> My means and manners never could attempt
> Above a hedge or haycock.   95

LIGONES.

> Sirrah, that quits not me. Where is this lady?

92–94. LIGONES. Sir . . . attempt]   Sir./ Bes. My . . . attempt Q1.
Q2; Lig. Sir . . . lie/ With . . .

---

78. *frozen*] used here as a general term of disapprobation, with
implications of coldness of spirit.
83. *yield*] reveal.
96. *quits*] requites.

Do that you do not use to do, tell truth,
Or, by my hand, I'll beat your captain's brains out,
Wash 'em, and put 'em in again, that will I.

BESSUS.

There was a lady, sir, I must confess,   100
Once in my charge; the Prince Tigranes gave her
To my guard for her safety. How I us'd her
She may herself report; she's with the prince now.
I did but wait upon her like a groom,
Which she will testify, I am sure. If not,   105
My brains are at your service when you please, sir,
And glad I have 'em for you.

LIGONES.

This is most likely; sir, I ask your pardon
And am sorry I was so intemperate.

BESSUS.

Well, I can ask no more. You would think it strange   110
Now to have me beat you at first sight.

LIGONES.

Indeed I would, but I know your goodness can
Forget twenty beatings. You must forgive me.

BESSUS.

Yes, there's my hand. Go where you will; I shall
Think you a valiant fellow for all this.   115

LIGONES [Aside].

My daughter is a whore;
I feel it now too sensible. Yet I will see her,
Discharge myself of being father to her,
And then back to my country and there die.—
Farewell, captain.

BESSUS.   Farewell, sir, farewell.   120
Commend me to the gentlewoman, I pray'ee.   *Exit* Ligones.

1 SWORDMAN.

How now, captain; bear up, man.

BESSUS.

Gentlemen o'th' sword, your hands once more.

121. S.D. *Exit* Ligones.] *after* cap-   captain, *l. 120 Q1.*
tain, *l. 120 Q2–8, F; Exit. after*

---

117. *sensible*] sensibly, forcibly.

I have been kick'd again, but the foolish fellow is penitent;
H'as ask'd me mercy, and my honor's safe.   125

2 SWORDMAN.

We knew that, or the foolish fellow had better
A' kick'd his grandsire.

BESSUS.   Confirm, confirm, I pray.

1 SWORDMAN.

There be our hands again.

2 SWORDMAN.   Now let him come
And say he was not sorry, and he sleeps for it.

BESSUS.

Alas, good, ignorant old man. Let him go,   130
Let him go; these courses will undo him.   *Exeunt.*

[V.ii]   *Enter* Ligones *and* Bacurius.

BACURIUS.

My lord, your authority is good, and I am glad it is so,
for my consent would never hinder you from seeing your
own king. I am a minister, but not a governor, of this
state. Yonder is your king; I'll leave you.   *Exit.*

                  Enter Tigranes *and* Spaconia.

LIGONES [*Aside*].

There he is, indeed, and with him my   5
Disloyal child.

TIGRANES [*To* Spaconia].   I do perceive my fault
So much that yet, methinks, thou shouldst not have
Forgiven me.

LIGONES.   Health to your majesty.

TIGRANES.

What? Good Ligones, welcome; what business
Brought thee hither?

LIGONES.   Several businesses.   10
My public business will appear by this. [*Gives him a paper.*]
I have a message to deliver, which,
If it please you so to authorize, is

127. S.P. BESSUS.] *Q2; om. Q1.*   4.1. *Enter . . .* Spaconia.] *Q2; after*
[V.ii]   indeed, *l. 5 Q1.*

An embassage from the Armenian state
Unto Arbaces for your liberty.   15
The offer's there set down; please you to read it.
TIGRANES.
There is no alteration happened since
I came thence?
LIGONES.   None, sir; all is as it was.
TIGRANES.
And all our friends are well?
LIGONES.   All very well.   [Tigranes *reads*.]
SPACONIA [*Aside*].
Though I have done nothing but what was good,   20
I dare not see my father; it was fault
Enough not to acquaint him with that good.
LIGONES.
Madam, I should have seen you.
SPACONIA.   Oh, good sir, forgive me.
LIGONES.
Forgive you! Why, I am no kin to you, am I?
SPACONIA.
Should it be measur'd by my mean deserts,   25
Indeed you are not.
LIGONES.   Thou couldst prate unhappily
Ere thou couldst go; would thou couldst do as well.
And how does your custom hold out here?
SPACONIA.   Sir?
LIGONES.   Are you
In private still, or how?
SPACONIA.   What do you mean?
LIGONES.
Do you take money? Are you come to sell sin yet? Perhaps   30
I can help you to liberal clients, or has not the king cast
you off yet? Oh, thou vile creature, whose best commenda-
tion is that thou art a young whore! I would thy mother
had liv'd to see this, or, rather, would I had died ere I
had seen it. Why didst not make me acquainted when   35
thou wert first resolv'd to be a whore? I would have seen
thy hot lust satisfied more privately. I would have kept a

_____

27. *go*] walk.   28. *custom*] business.

dancer and a whole consort of musicians in mine own
house only to fiddle thee.

SPACONIA.

Sir, I was never whore.

LIGONES.   If thou couldst not   40
Say so much for thyself, thou shouldst be carted.

TIGRANES.

Ligones, I have read it and like it;
You shall deliver it.

LIGONES.   Well, sir, I will.
But I have private business with you.

TIGRANES.   Speak; what is't?

LIGONES.

How has my age deserv'd so ill of you,   45
That you can pick no strumpets in the land
But out of my breed?

TIGRANES.   Strumpets, good Ligones?

LIGONES.

Yes, and I wish to have you know I scorn
To get a whore for any prince alive,
And yet scorn will not help, methinks. My daughter   50
Might have been spar'd; there were enough beside.

TIGRANES.

May I not prosper but she's innocent
As morning light for me, and, I dare swear,
For all the world.

LIGONES.   Why is she with you then?
Can she wait on you better than your men?   55
Has she a gift in plucking off your stockings?
Can she make caudles well or cut your corns?
Why do you keep her with you? For your queen
I know you do contemn her; so should I,

---

38. *consort*] company.
41. *carted*] shamed by being driven through the streets in an open
cart, a punishment traditionally accorded prostitutes and bawds.
53. *for me*] insofar as I am concerned.
57. *caudles*] "Warm drink[s] consisting of thin gruel, mixed with
wine or ale, sweetened and spiced, given chiefly to sick people. . . ."
(*OED, sb.* 1).
59. *contemn*] scorn.

And every subject else think much at it.   60

TIGRANES.

Let 'em think much, but 'tis more firm than earth
Thou seest thy queen there.

LIGONES.

Then have I made a fair hand; I call'd her "whore." If
I shall speak now as her father, I cannot choose but
greatly rejoice that she shall be a queen. But if I should   65
speak to you as a statesman, she were more fit to be your
whore.

TIGRANES.

Get you about your business to Arbaces;
Now you talk idly.

LIGONES.   Yes, sir, I will go.

And shall she be a queen? She had more wit   70
Than her old father when she ran away.
Shall she be a queen? Now, by my troth, 'tis fine.
I'll dance out of all measure at her wedding.
Shall I not, sir?

TIGRANES.   Yes, marry, shalt thou.

LIGONES.

I'll make these wither'd kexes bear my body   75
Two hours together above ground.

TIGRANES.   Nay, go;
My business requires haste.

LIGONES.   Good God preserve you;
You are an excellent king.

SPACONIA.   Farewell, good father.

LIGONES.

Farewell, sweet, virtuous daughter.
I never was so joyful in my life,   80
That I remember. Shall she be a queen?
Now I perceive a man may weep for joy;
I had thought they had lied that said so.   *Exit.*

TIGRANES.

Come, my dear love.

---

63. *made . . . hand*] done well (ironically).

73. *out . . . measure*] immoderately, with a pun on "measure," a
dance with a deliberate and stately rhythm.

75. *kexes*] hollow stalks (i.e., legs).

SPACONIA.   But you may see another
   May alter that again.
TIGRANES.   Urge it no more;   85
   I have made up a new strong constancy
   Not to be shook with eyes. I know I have
   The passions of a man, but if I meet
   With any subject that shall hold my eyes
   More firmly than is fit, I'll think of thee   90
   And run away from it. Let that suffice.   *Exeunt.*

[V.iii]   *Enter* Bacurius *and a* Servant.

BACURIUS.
   Three gentlemen without to speak with me?
SERVANT.   Yes, sir.
BACURIUS.
   Let them come in.
SERVANT.   They are enter'd, sir, already.

                Enter Bessus *and* Swordmen.

BACURIUS.
   Now, fellows, your business. [*To* Servant] Are these the
      gentlemen?
BESSUS.
   My lord, I have made bold to bring these gentlemen,
   My friends o'th' sword, along with me.
BACURIUS.   I am   5
   Afraid you'll fight then.
BESSUS.   My good lord, I will not;
   Your lordship is mistaken. Fear not, lord.
BACURIUS.
   Sir, I am sorry for't.
BESSUS.
   I can ask no more in honor.—Gentlemen,
   You hear my lord is sorry.
BACURIUS.   Not that I have   10
   Beaten you, but beaten one that will be beaten,

---

   87. *with eyes*] by sight.
[V.iii]
   1. *without*] outside.

One whose dull body will require a lancing,
As surfeits do the diet, spring and fall.
Now to your swordmen:
What come they for, good Captain Stockfish?   15

BESSUS.

It seems your lordship has forgot my name.

BACURIUS.

No, nor your nature neither, though they are
Things fitter, I confess, for anything
Than my remembrance or any honest man's.
What shall these billets do, be pil'd up in my woodyard?   20

BESSUS.

Your lordship holds your mirth still; God continue it.
But, for these gentlemen, they come—

BACURIUS.   —To swear
You are a coward. Spare your book; I do believe it.

BESSUS.

Your lordship still draws wide; they come to vouch
Under their valiant hands I am no coward.   25

BACURIUS.

That would be a show indeed worth seeing. Sirrah, be
wise and take money for this motion; travel with it, and
where the name of Bessus has been known or a good
coward stirring 'twill yield more than a tilting. This will
prove more beneficial to you, if you be thrifty, than your   30
captainship and more natural.—Men of most valiant
hands, is this true?

2 SWORDMAN.

It is so, most renowned.

BACURIUS.

'Tis somewhat strange.

1 SWORDMAN.   Lord, it is strange, yet true.

12. a] *Q2; om. Q1.*   34. S.P. BACURIUS.] *Q2; om. Q1.*
13. fall] *Q2;* full *Q1.*

---

13. *surfeits*] overindulgences, or the morbid conditions caused by
them.
15. *Stockfish*] a dried fish, made tender by beating.
20. *billets*] logs (i.e., the swordmen).
23. *book*] i.e., the Bible, on which the oath would be taken.
24. *draws wide*] misunderstands.
27. *motion*] puppet-show.

We have examined, from your lordship's foot there   35
To this man's head, the nature of the beatings,
And we do find his honor is come off
Clean and sufficient. This as our swords shall help us.

BACURIUS.

You are much bound to your bilbo-men; I am glad you
are straight again, captain. 'Twere good you would think   40
some way to gratify them. They have undergone a labor
for you, Bessus, would have puzzl'd Hercules with all his
valor.

2 SWORDMAN.

Your lordship must understand we are no men
O'th' law, that take pay for our opinions.   45
It is sufficient we have clear'd our friend.

BACURIUS.

Yet here is something due which I, as touch'd
In conscience, will discharge, captain. I'll pay
This rent for you.

BESSUS.   Spare yourself, my good lord.
My brave friends aim at nothing but the virtue.   50

BACURIUS.

That's but a cold discharge, sir, for their pains.

2 SWORDMAN.

O Lord, my good lord!

BACURIUS.

Be not so modest; I will give you something.

BESSUS.

They shall dine with your lordship; that's sufficient.

BACURIUS.

Something in hand the while.—Ye rogues! Ye apple-squires!   55
Do you come hither with your bottled valor,
You windy froth, to limit out my beatings?   [Kicks them.]

57. You] Your Q1–8, F.

---

39. *bilbo-men*] swordmen, bullies (from Bilbao, a Spanish city noted
for the high quality of the swords manufactured there).
49. *rent*] debt, charge.
55. *the while*] meanwhile.
55. *apple-squires*] pimps.
57. *You windy froth*] Modern editions concur with the early in
reading *Your*, which puts *froth* in apposition to *valor* (1. 56). But *your*
is an easy misreading for *you* or, in this instance, an easy mistake of

1 SWORDMAN.

    I do beseech your lordship—

2 SWORDMAN.   Oh, good lord—

BACURIUS.

    'Sfoot, what a many of beaten slaves are here!—

    Get me a cudgel, sirrah, and a tough one. [*Exit* Servant.]   60

2 SWORDMAN.

    More of your foot, I do beseech your lordship.

BACURIUS.

    You shall, you shall, dog, and your fellow beagle.

1 SWORDMAN.

    O' this side, good my lord.

BACURIUS.   Off with your swords,

    For if you hurt my foot, I'll have you flay'd,

    You rascals.

1 SWORDMAN.   Mine's off, my lord.

2 SWORDMAN.   I beseech   65

    Your lordship stay a little; my strap's tied

    To my codpiece point. Now, when you please.

BACURIUS.

    Captain, these are your valiant friends. You long

    For a little too?

BESSUS.   I am very well,

    I humbly thank your lordship.

BACURIUS.   What's that in   70

    Your pocket, slave? My key, you mongrel? Thy

    Buttocks cannot be so hard; out with't quickly.

2 SWORDMAN.

    Here 'tis, sir; a small piece of artillery   [*Hands him a pistol.*]

    That a gentleman, a dear friend of your lordship's,

    Sent me with to get it mended, sir,   75

    For if you mark, the nose is somewhat loose.

BACURIUS.

    A friend of mine, you rascal!—I was never

---

memory caused by *your* in l. 56. *Froth,* although a possible renaming
of *valor* in this situation, makes better sense as a term of abuse, like
"scum" (cf. *OED, sb.* 3).

    59. *many*] crowd.

    67. *codpiece point*] a lace by means of which the codpiece, the
bagged appendage to the front of the breeches, was fastened to the hose.

Wearier of doing nothing than
Kicking these two footballs.

Enter Servant.

SERVANT.
    Here's a good cudgel, sir.
BACURIUS.   It comes too late.   80
    I am weary; prithee do thou beat 'em.
2 SWORDMAN.
    My lord, this is foul play, i'faith, to put
    A fresh man upon us; men are but men.
BACURIUS.
    That jest shall save your bones. [*To* Bessus] Up with
    your rotten regiment and be gone.—I had rather thresh   85
    than be bound to kick these rascals till they cried hold.—
    Bessus, you may put your hand to them now, and then
    you are quit.—Farewell; as you like this, pray visit me
    again. 'Twill keep me in good breath.   *Exit* Bacurius.
2 SWORDMAN.
    H'as a devilish hard foot; I never felt the like.   90
1 SWORDMAN.
    Nor I, and yet I'm sure I ha' felt a hundred.
2 SWORDMAN.
    If he kick thus i'th' dog days, he will be dry founder'd.—
    What cure now, captain, besides oil of bays?

79.1. *Enter* Servant.] *Q3; om. Q1;*   89. S.D. *Exit* Bacurius.] *Q2; om.*
Enter Servant, Will. Adkinson: Q2.   Q1.

---

78. *nothing*] anything.
88. *quit*] released from your debt.
92. *dog days*] the hottest days of the year, in England most of July
and early to middle August, when the Dog Star is above the horizon.
92. *dry founder'd*] lamed. The founder is a disease usually of the
feet and legs, sometimes of the chest muscles, of animals, chiefly horses
(*OED, sb.*⁶). Probably the reference here is to what today is called
"laminitis," an inflammation of the sensitive tissue inside the wall of
a horse's hoof, which may be brought on in hot weather by concussion.
The term "dry" apparently distinguishes foundering of this kind from
"foundering in the body," of which an eruption was symptomatic. **Cf.**
Bartholomew Fair, ed. E. A. Horsman (1960), II.iii.54 and note.
93. *oil of bays*] a liniment made from bayberries.

BESSUS.

Why, well enough, I warrant you. You can go?

2 SWORDMAN.

Yes, God be thanked. But I feel a shrewd ache;   95
Sure, he has sprang my huckle bone.

1 SWORDMAN.   I ha' lost a haunch.

BESSUS.

A little butter, friend, a little butter;
Butter and parsley is a sovereign matter.
Probatum est.

2 SWORDMAN.   Captain, we must request
Your hands now to our honors.

BESSUS.   Yes, marry, shall ye,   100
And then let all the world come; we are valiant
To ourselves, and there's an end.

1 SWORDMAN.   Nay, then we must
Be valiant.—Oh my ribs!

2 SWORDMAN.   Oh my small guts!
A plague upon these sharp-toed shoes; they are murderers.

                                                                Exeunt.

[V.iv]   *Enter* Arbaces *with his sword drawn.*

ARBACES.

It is resolv'd. I bore it whilst I could;
I can no more. Hell, open all thy gates,
And I will through them; if they be shut,
I'll batter 'em, but I will find the place
Where the most damn'd have dwelling. Ere I end,   5
Amongst them all they shall not have a sin
But I may call it mine. I must begin
With murder of my friend, and so go on
To an incestuous ravishing, and end
My life and sins with a forbidden blow   10
Upon myself.

---

94. *go*] walk.
96. *huckle bone*] hipbone.
98. *sovereign matter*] a very good medicine.
99. *Probatum est*] it has been tried, proved.

Enter Mardonius.

MARDONIUS.   What tragedy is near?
That hand was never wont to draw a sword
But it cried dead to something.
ARBACES.   Mardonius,
Have you bid Gobrius come?
MARDONIUS.   How do you, sir?
ARBACES.
Well. Is he coming?
MARDONIUS.   Why, sir, are you thus?   15
Why does your hand proclaim a lawless war
Against yourself?
ARBACES.
Thou answerest me one question with another.
Is Gobrius coming?
MARDONIUS.   Sir, he is.
ARBACES.   'Tis well;
I can forbear your questions then. Begone.   20
MARDONIUS.
Sir, I have mark'd—
ARBACES.
Mark less; it troubles you and me.
MARDONIUS.   —You are
More variable than you were.
ARBACES.   It may be so.
MARDONIUS.
Today no hermit could be humblier
Than you were to us all.
ARBACES.   And what of this?   25
MARDONIUS.
And now you take new rage into your eyes,
As you would look us all out of the land.
ARBACES.
I do confess it; will that satisfy?
I prithee, get thee gone.

20–21. I . . . mark'd—] *Q2; Mar.   Q1.*
I. . . . Begone./ Sir . . . mark'd—

---

12. *wont*] accustomed.
20. *forbear*] do without.

MARDONIUS.

Sir, I will speak.

ARBACES.   Will ye?

MARDONIUS.   It is my duty;   30
I fear you will kill yourself. I am a subject,
And you shall do me wrong in't. 'Tis my cause,
And I may speak.

ARBACES.   Thou art not train'd in sin,
It seems, Mardonius. Kill myself? By heaven,
I will not do it yet, and, when I will,   35
I'll tell thee. Then I shall be such a creature
That thou wilt give me leave without a word.
There is a method in man's wickedness;
It grows up by degrees. I am not come
So high as killing of myself; there are   40
A hundred thousand sins 'twixt me and it
Which I must do. I shall come to't at last,
But, take my oath, not now. Be satisfied,
And get thee hence.

MARDONIUS.

I am sorry 'tis so ill.

ARBACES.   Be sorry then.   45
True sorrow is alone; grieve by thyself.

MARDONIUS.

I pray you, let me see your sword put up
Before I go. I'll leave you then.

ARBACES.   Why, so!   [*Puts up his sword.*]
What folly is this in thee! Is it not
As apt to mischief as it was before?   50
Can I not reach it, thinkest thou? These are toys
For children to be pleas'd with and not men.
Now I am safe, you think. I would the book
Of fate were here. My sword is not so sure
But I should get it out and mangle that,   55
That all the destinies should quite forget

36. thee. Then] *Dyce*; thee then:
Q1–8, F.

---

32. *in't*] i.e., by killing yourself.
51. *toys*] frivolous things.   54. *sure*] secure.

Their fix'd decrees and haste to make us new,
Far-other fortunes. Mine could not be worse.
Wilt thou now leave me?

MARDONIUS.

God put into your bosom temperate thoughts.   60
I'll leave you though I fear.

ARBACES.   Go; thou art honest.   *Exit* Mardonius.
Why should the hasty errors of my youth
Be so unpardonable, to draw a sin
Helpless upon me?

Enter Gobrius.

GOBRIUS [*Aside*].   There is the king.
Now it is ripe.

ARBACES.   Draw near, thou guilty man,   65
That art the author of the loathed'st crime
Five ages have brought forth, and hear me speak.
Curses incurable and all the evils
Man's body or his spirit can receive
Be with thee.

GOBRIUS.   Why, sir, do you curse me thus?   70

ARBACES.

Why do I curse thee? If there be a man
Subtle in curses, that exceeds the rest,
His worst wish on thee. Thou hast broke my heart.

GOBRIUS.

How, sir! Have I preserv'd you from a child
From all the arrows malice or ambition   75
Could shoot at you, and have I this for pay?

ARBACES.

'Tis true thou didst preserve me and in that
Wert crueler than harden'd murderers
Of infants and their mothers; thou didst save me
Only till thou hadst studied out a way   80
How to destroy me cunningly thyself.
This was a curious way of torturing.

61. S.D. *Exit* Mardonius.] *Q3; after*
fear *Q2; Exit. after* fear *Q1.*

82. *curious*] subtle.

GOBRIUS.

What do you mean?

ARBACES.

Thou know'st the evils thou hast done to me.
Dost thou remember all those witching letters   85
Thou sent'st unto me to Armenia
Fill'd with the praise of my beloved sister,
Where thou extol'st her beauty? What had I
To do with that? What could her beauty be
To me? And thou didst write how well she lov'd me—   90
Dost thou remember this?—so that I doted
Something before I saw her.

GOBRIUS.   This is true.

ARBACES.

Is it? And when I was return'd, thou know'st
Thou didst pursue it till thou wound'st me in
To such a strange and unbeliev'd affection   95
As good men cannot think on.

GOBRIUS.   This I grant;
I think I was the cause.

ARBACES.   Wert thou? Nay, more,
I think thou meant'st it.

GOBRIUS.   Sir, I hate a lie
As I love God and honesty; I did.
It was my meaning.

ARBACES.   Be thine own sad judge;   100
A further condemnation will not need.
Prepare thyself to die.

GOBRIUS.   Why, sir, to die?

ARBACES.

Why wouldst thou live? Was ever yet offender
So impudent that had a thought of mercy
After confession of a crime like this?   105
Get out I cannot where thou hurl'st me in,
But I can take revenge; that's all the sweetness

93. And when] *Q2*; and I when *Q1*.   94–95. in/ To] *Q2*; into *Q1*.

95. *unbeliev'd*] incredible.
100. *sad*] sober.

Left for me.

GOBRIUS [*Aside*].   Now is the time.—Hear me but speak.

ARBACES.

No. Yet I will be far more merciful
Than thou wert to me. Thou didst steal into me   110
And never gavest me warning; so much time
As I give thee now had prevented thee
Forever. Notwithstanding all thy sins,
If thou hast hope that there is yet a prayer
To save thee, turn and speak it to yourself.   115

GOBRIUS.

Sir, you shall know your sins before you do 'em.
If you kill me—

ARBACES.   I will not stay then.

GOBRIUS.   —Know
You kill your father.

ARBACES.   How?

GOBRIUS.   You kill your father.

ARBACES.

My father! Though I know it for a lie
Made out of fear to save thy stained life,   120
The very reverence of the word comes cross me
And ties mine arm down.

GOBRIUS.   I will tell you that
Shall heighten you again. I am thy father;
I charge thee hear me.

ARBACES.   If it should be so,
As 'tis most false, and that I should be found   125
A bastard issue, the despised fruit
Of lawless lust, I should no more admire
All my wild passions. But another truth
Shall be wrung from thee. If I could come by
The spirit of pain, it should be pour'd on thee   130
Till thou allowest thyself more full of lies
Than he that teaches thee.

Enter Arane.

---

127. *admire*] wonder at.   130. *spirit*] essence.
132. *he . . . thee*] i.e., Satan, Father of Lies.

ARANE.   Turn thee about.
    I come to speak to thee, thou wicked man;
    Hear me, thou tyrant.
ARBACES.   I will turn to thee.
    Hear me, thou strumpet. I have blotted out   135
    The name of mother as thou hast thy shame.
ARANE.
    My shame! Thou hast less shame than anything.
    Why dost thou keep my daughter in a prison?
    Why dost thou call her sister and do this?
ARBACES.
    Cease, thou strange impudence, and answer quickly.   140
    If thou contemn'st me,   *Draws his sword.*
                    this will ask an answer.
    And have it.
ARANE.   Help me, gentle Gobrius.
ARBACES.
    Guilt dare not help guilt: though they grow together
    In doing ill, yet at the punishment
    They sever and each flies the noise of other.   145
    Think not of help—answer.
ARANE.   I will; to what?
ARBACES.
    To such a thing as, if it be a truth,
    Think what a creature thou hast made thyself
    That didst not shame to do what I must blush
    Only to ask thee. Tell me who I am,   150
    Whose son I am, without all circumstance.
    Be thou as hasty as my sword will be
    If thou refusest.
ARANE.   Why, you are his son.
ARBACES.
    His son? Swear; swear, thou worse than woman damn'd.
ARANE.
    By all that's good, you are.

141. S.D. *Draws . . . sword.*] *Q8;*
om. *Q1-7, F.*

---

141. *contemn'st*] scorn.   151. *all circumstance*] any detail.

ARBACES.   Then art thou all   155
 That ever was known bad. Now is the cause
 Of all my strange misfortunes come to light.
 What reverence expect'st thou from a child
 To bring forth which thou hast offended heaven,
 Thy husband, and the land? Adulterous witch,   160
 I know now why thou wouldst have poison'd me;
 I was thy lust which thou wouldst have forgot.
 Thou wicked mother of my sins and me,
 Show me the way to the inheritance
 I have by thee, which is a spacious world   165
 Of impious acts, that I may soon possess it.
 Plagues rot thee as thou liv'st, and such diseases
 As use to pay lust recompense thy deed.

GOBRIUS.
 You do not know why you curse thus.

ARBACES.   Too well.
 You are a pair of vipers, and behold   170
 The serpent you have got. There is no beast,
 But, if he knew it, has a pedigree
 As brave as mine, for they have more descents,
 And I am every way as beastly got,
 As far without the compass of a law,   175
 As they.

ARANE. You spend your rage and words in vain
 And rail upon a guess. Hear us a little.

ARBACES.
 No, I will never hear, but talk away
 My breath and die.

GOBRIUS.   Why, but you are no bastard.

ARBACES.
 How's that?

158. expect'st] *Q4*; expects *Q1, 3*;
expectes *Q2*.

---

 171. *got*] begotten.
 173. *brave*] worthy.
 173. *descents*] offspring.
 174. *got*] begotten.

ARANE.   Nor child of mine.

ARBACES.   Still you go on   180
    In wonders to me.

GOBRIUS.   Pray you be more patient;
    I may bring comfort to you.

ARBACES.   I will kneel
    And hear with the obedience of a child.
    Good father, speak; I do acknowledge you,
    So you bring comfort.   185

GOBRIUS.
    First know, our last king, your supposed father,
    Was old and feeble when he married her
    And almost all the land, as she, past hope
    Of issue from him.

ARBACES.   Therefore, she took leave
    To play the whore because the king was old.   190
    Is this the comfort?

ARANE.   What will you find out
    To give me satisfaction when you find
    How you have injur'd me? Let fire consume me,
    If ever I were whore.

GOBRIUS.   Forbear these starts,
    Or I will leave you wedded to despair   195
    As you are now. If you can find a temper,
    My breath shall be a pleasant western wind
    That cools and blasts not.

ARBACES.   Bring it out, good father;
    I'll lie and listen here as reverently
    As to an angel. If I breathe too loud,   200
    Tell me, for I would be as still as night.

GOBRIUS.
    Our king, I say, was old, and this our queen
    Desired to bring an heir, but yet her husband,
    She thought, was past it and to be dishonest

181. you] *Q2; om. Q1.*

---

194. *Forbear*] abstain from.
203. *bring*] bring forth.
204. *dishonest*] unchaste.

I think she would not; if she would have been,   205
The truth is she was watch'd so narrowly
And had so slender opportunity
She hardly could have been. But yet her cunning
Found out this way: she feign'd herself with child;
And posts were sent in haste throughout the land,   210
And God was humbly thank'd in every church,
That so had bless'd the queen, and prayers were made
For her safe going and delivery.
She feign'd now to grow bigger; and perceiv'd
This hope of issue made her fear'd and brought   215
A far more large respect from every man,
And saw her power increase and was resolv'd,
Since she believ'd she could not hav't indeed,
At least she would be thought to have a child.

ARBACES.

Do I not hear it well? Nay, I will make   220
No noise at all, but pray you to the point
Quick as you can.

GOBRIUS.   Now when the time was full
She should be brought abed, I had a son
Born, which was you. This the queen hearing of
Mov'd me to let her have you, and such reasons   225
She showed me as she knew would tie
My secrecy—she sware you should be king.
And, to be short, I did deliver you
Unto her and pretended you were dead,
And in mine own house kept a funeral   230
And had an empty coffin put in earth.
That night the queen feign'd hastily to labor,
And, by a pair of women of her own
Which she had charm'd, she made the world believe
She was deliver'd of you. You grew up   235
As the king's son till you were six year old.
Then did the king die and did leave to me

---

213. *going*] carrying of the child (cf. *OED, v.* 7).
215. *fear'd*] revered.
227. *sware*] i.e., swore.
234. *charm'd*] strongly influenced.

> Protection of the realm and, contrary
> To his own expectation, left this queen
> Truly with child indeed of the fair Princess   240
> Panthea. Then she could have torn her hair
> And did alone to me, yet durst not speak
> In public, for she knew she should be found
> A traitor and her talk would have been thought
> Madness or anything rather than truth.   245
> This was the only cause why she did seek
> To poison you, and I to keep you safe,
> And this the reason why I sought to kindle
> Some spark of love in you to fair Panthea,
> That she might get part of her right again.   250

ARBACES.
> And have you made an end now; is this all?
> If not, I will be still till I am aged,
> Till all my hairs are silver.

GOBRIUS.   This is all.

ARBACES.
> And is it true, say you too, madam?   [*Rises.*]

ARANE.   Yes,
> God knows it is most true.   255

ARBACES.
> Panthea, then, is not my sister?

GOBRIUS.   No.

ARBACES.
> But can you prove this?

GOBRIUS.   If you will give consent,
> Else who dare go about it?

ARBACES.   Give consent!
> Why, I will have them all that know it rack'd
> To get this from 'em.—All that wait'st without,   260
> Come in; whate'er you be, come in and be

---

254. too] *Q2; om. Q1.*   260. wait'st] waites *Q1–2;* waits
257. S.P. GOBRIUS.] *Q2; om. Q1.*   *Q3–8,* wait *F.*

---

258. *Else . . . it?*] Who else dare be concerned with the matter?
259. *rack'd*] tortured (cf. IV.ii.186).
261. *whate'er you be*] whoever you are, regardless of your station or condition.

Partakers of my joy!

Enter Mardonius, Bessus, [*the two* Gentlemen,] *and others.*

                    Oh, you are welcome.
Mardonius, the best news—nay, draw no nearer;
They all shall hear it—I am found no king!
MARDONIUS.
    Is that so good news?
ARBACES.   Yes, the happiest news   265
    That e'er was heard.
MARDONIUS.   Indeed, 'twere well for you
    If you might be a little less obey'd.
ARBACES.
    One call the queen.
MARDONIUS.   Why, she is there.
ARBACES.   The queen,
Mardonius. Panthea is the queen,
And I am plain Arbaces.—Go some one;   270
She is in Gobrius' house.   *Exit* 1 Gentleman.
               Since I saw you
There are a thousand things deliver'd to me
You little dream of.
MARDONIUS.   So it should seem.—My lord,
    What fury's this?
GOBRIUS.   Believe me, 'tis no fury;
    All that he says is truth.
MARDONIUS.   'Tis very strange.   275
ARBACES.
    Why do you keep your hats off, gentlemen?
    Is it to me? I swear it must not be.
    Nay, trust me; in good faith, it must not be.
    I cannot now command you, but I pray you,

---

262. S.D. *Enter . . . others.*] *after*
welcome *Q1–8, F.*
265. so] *Q2; om. Q1.*
268. One] *Q2;* On, *Q1.*

271. S.D. *Exit* 1 Gentleman.] *Dyce;*
Exit a Gent. after of, *l. 273 Q2–8,*
F; om. Q1.
277–278. I . . . me;] *Q2; om. Q1.*

---

272. *deliver'd*] spoken, revealed.
274. *fury*] frenzy.

For the respect you bare me when you took   280
Me for your king, each man clap on his hat
At my desire.

MARDONIUS.   We will, but you are not found
So mean a man but that you may be cover'd
As well as we, may you not?

ARBACES.   Oh, not here;
You may but not I, for here is my father   285
In presence.

MARDONIUS. Where?

ARBACES.   Why, there. Oh, the whole story
Would be a wilderness to lose thyself
Forever.—Oh, pardon me, dear father,
For all the idle and unreverent words
That I have spoke in idle moods to you.—   290
I am Arbaces; we all fellow-subjects;
Nor is the queen, Panthea, now my sister.

BESSUS.

Why, if you remember, fellow-subject Arbaces, I told you
once she was not your sister; I said she look'd nothing
like you.   295

ARBACES.

I think you did, good Captain Bessus.

BESSUS [*Aside*].

Here will arise another question now amongst the swordmen, whether I be to call him to account for beating me
now he's prov'd no king.

Enter Ligones.

MARDONIUS.

Sir, here's Ligones, the agent for the Armenian state.   300

ARBACES.

Where is he?—I know your business, good Ligones.

LIGONES.

We must have our king again, and will.

294. I said] I say *Q1*; I, and 300. state] *Q2*; king *Q1*.
Q2–8, F.

280. *bare*] i.e., bore.

ARBACES.

    I knew that was your business. You shall have
    Your king again and have him so again
    As never king was had.—Go, one of you,   305
    And bid Bacurius bring Tigranes hither
    And bring the lady with him that Panthea—
    The queen, Panthea—sent me word this morning
    Was brave Tigranes' mistress.   *Exit* 2 Gentleman.

LIGONES.   'Tis Spaconia.

ARBACES.

    Ay, ay, Spaconia.

LIGONES.   She is my daughter.   310

ARBACES.

    She is so; I could now tell anything
    I never heard. Your king shall go so home
    As never man went.

MARDONIUS.   Shall he go on's head?

ARBACES.

    He shall have chariots easier than air
    That I will have invented, and ne'er think   315
    He shall pay any ransom; and thyself,
    That art the messenger, shall ride before him
    On a horse cut out of an entire diamond
    That shall be made to go with golden wheels,
    I know not how yet.

LIGONES [*Aside*].   Why, I shall be made   320
    Forever; they belied this king with us
    And said he was unkind.

ARBACES.   And then thy daughter—
    She shall have some strange thing; we'll have the kingdom
    Sold utterly and put into a toy
    Which she shall wear about her carelessly   325
    Somewhere or other.

---

309. S.D. *Exit* 2 Gentleman.] *Q2*   323. thing] *Q2*; thinke *Q1*.
(. . . two . . .); *om. Q1.*

---

311. *She is so*] yes, of course she is.
323. *strange*] rare, unusual.
324. *toy*] trinket.

Enter Panthea *and* 1 Gentleman.

See the virtuous queen!—
Behold the humblest subject that you have
Kneel here before you.

PANTHEA. Why kneel you to me
That am your vassal?

ARBACES. Grant me one request.

PANTHEA.

Alas, what can I grant you? What I can,   330
I will.

ARBACES. That you will please to marry me,
If I can prove it lawful.

PANTHEA. Is that all?
More willingly than I would draw this air.

ARBACES.

I'll kiss this hand in earnest.

Enter Bacurius *and* 2 Gentleman.

BACURIUS. Sir, Tigranes

326. S.D. *Enter . . . Gentleman.*]   *om. Q1–8, F.*
after you, *l. 328* Q2; *Enter Pan.*   334. S.P. BACURIUS.] *Dyce sugges-*
after queen!— *Q1.*   *tion; Mar.* Q1; 2 *Gent.* Q2–8, F.
334. S.D. *Enter . . . Gentleman.*]

334. *in earnest*] (1) as a pledge, (2) seriously.
334. S.D. *Bacurius*] Q1 here omits the stage direction and assigns
the speech beginning "Sir, Tigranes" to Mardonius, an obviously unsatisfactory arrangement because Mardonius, who is on stage from his
entrance at V.iv.262, would have no way of knowing Tigranes' objec-
tions to seeing Panthea. Q2 also omits the stage direction, but improves
matters somewhat by giving the speech to the Second Gentleman, who
in that text had been sent for Tigranes at l. 309. Dyce, however, noting
that at ll. 305–306 Arbaces commands, "Go, one of you,/ And bid Bacurius bring Tigranes hither," suggests that Bacurius comes on at this point
and delivers the speech and that the Second Gentleman enters at l. 337
with Tigranes and Spaconia. This idea is attractive, not only because
it conforms with Arbaces' order but also because it seems odd that
Bacurius would have been excluded from the gathering of all the
courtly characters at the end of the play. Yet Q2 must have gotten the
speech prefix "2 *Gent.*" from somewhere, and it seems more probable
that the words would have been mistakenly printed as such if they
stood in an annotation as the last of a stage direction in a form similar

Is coming, though he made it strange at first 335
To see the princess any more.

ARBACES. The queen,

Thou meanest.

Enter Tigranes *and* Spaconia.

Oh, my Tigranes, pardon me.
Tread on my neck; I freely offer it,
And if thou beest so given. Take revenge,
For I have injur'd thee.

TIGRANES. No, I forgive 340
And rejoice more that you have found repentance
Than I my liberty.

ARBACES. Mayst thou be happy
In thy fair choice, for thou art temperate.
You owe no ransom to the state, know that.
I have a thousand joys to tell you of 345
Which yet I dare not utter till I pay
My thanks to heaven for 'em. Will you go
With me and help me? Pray you do.

TIGRANES. I will.

ARBACES.

Take then your fair one with you.—And you, queen
Of goodness and of us, oh, give me leave 350
To take your arm in mine.—Come everyone
That takes delight in goodness; help to sing
Loud thanks for me, that I am prov'd no king. [*Exeunt.*]

FINIS.

---

335. at first] Q2; om. Q1. l. 336 Q2–8, F.
337. S.D. *Enter . . . Spaconia.*] 349. And you] *F;* and your *Q1–7.*
after queen, l. *336 Q1; after* more,

---

to that adopted here than if they stood with the stage direction at
l. 337. It may be objected that Tigranes and Spaconia, who technically
are still prisoners, would not enter unaccompanied, but they are only a
few steps behind.

335. *made it strange*] was unwilling.
339. *And if*] if.

Appendix A

Historical Collation of Early Editions

The following notes list the substantive variations of Q1 (1619), Q2 (1625), Q3 (1631), Q4 (1639), Q5 (1655), Q6 (1661), Q7 (1676), F (1679), and Q8 (1693) from the text of this edition. Semi-substantive variations are excluded, and spellings are modernized, except in a few cases where the old spelling helps to show the relationship between variants. Omission of a siglum after the bracket indicates that the reading of the edition in question agrees with the text.

[I.i]
0.1. *Enter . . . Bessus.*] *Enter Mardonius and Bessus, two Captains.* Q2–8, F
1. h'as] he has Q2–8, F.
6. had as] had's Q2.
10. them] 'em Q2–8, F.
11. thou art] thou'rt Q2–8, F.
13. an] if Q2–8, F.
15. see't] see'r Q6.
16. with me] wi' me Q2–8, F.
17. wink'st] winkedst Q7–8, F.
18. strake] struck Q2–8, F.
25. I am] I'm Q2–8, F.
27. of his] of's Q2–8, F.
29. cruddles] curdles Q3–7, F.
29. wouldst] couldst Q2–8, F.
30. in this] i' this Q2–8, F.
33. venter] venture F.
33. for it] for't Q2–8, F.
34. venter] venture F.
34. good] *om.* Q2–8, F.
35. it is] 'tis Q2–8, F.
38. I fam'd] Fam'd Q2–8, F.
39. I am very] I'm e'en Q2–8, F.
40. o'th'] to th' Q2–8, F.
40. is] *om.* Q2–8.
43. them] 'em Q2–8, F.

46. of] on Q7–8.
47. in shifting a] of shifting of a Q3–6, F.
53. Bessus'] At Bessus' Q2–8, F.
56. Prithee] Pray thee Q2–8, F.
57. soldier] soldiers Q3–6, F.
58. merrily] meerely Q1.
60. composition] comparison Q5; compassion Q6.
63. away] a way Q5, 8.
67. not I] I not Q3–6, F.
69. meant'st] mean'st Q1, 4–6, 8; meanedst F.
81. come] *om.* Q2–8, F.
82. com'st] cam'st Q2–8, F.
86. extremities] extremity Q2–8, F.
88. the] his Q2–8, F.
88.1. *Enter . . . attendants.*] *Enter Arbaces and Tigranes, with attendants.* Q1; *Enter &c. Senet Flourish./ Enter* Arbaces *and* Tigranes *two Kings, &c./ The two Gentlemen.* Q2, 7–8; *. . . Kings and two Gentlemen.* Q3–6, F.
90. full] fall Q1.
105. year] years Q4–6, 8, F.
113. S.P. TIGRANES.] *om.* Q1.
113. Is it] Is't Q2–8, F.

115. Arbaces'] Arbace Q5–6, F.
116. talk'd, for in] talked, sir, in Q2–8, F.
125. Far] Fare Q5–6.
128. With] By Q2–8, F.
135. no] nay Q2–8, F.
139. an] any Q3–6, F.
140. god] good Q2–6; good man F.
143. It's] 'Tis Q2–8, F.
148. spoke] spake Q2–8, F.
148. not me] me not Q2–8, F.
161. are] have Q2–8, F.
169. for her] her for Q2, 7–8.
169. take] taste Q3–6, F.
178. one] owne Q1.
179. Would] Could Q2–8, F.
179. had] were Q7–8.
180. for] her Q1.
181. times] lives Q2–8, F.
189. fight] sight F.
196. Iberia] *Ileria* Q1.
200. two] to Q2–8, F.
204. S.D. *Exeunt* Tigranes.] *Exe*: after l. 203 Q1; *Exit Tigranes.* after l. 203 Q2–8, F.
207. done] *om.* Q2, 7–8; done't Q3–4; don't Q5–6, F.
219. if't] if Q2–8, F.
220. with you] wi' you Q2–6, F.
221. have] ha Q2–8, F.
221. stunk] sunke Q1.
221. o'th'] of o'th' Q2.
228. -royal] *om.* Q1.
228. about's] about his Q2, 7–8; down Q3–6, F.
229. didst thou learn that] learn'st that Q2–6; learn'st thou that Q7; learn'st thou F, Q8.
230. Puft] Pish Q2–8, F.
230. I not] not I Q2–8, F.
231. Talk'd] Talk Q1–6.
232. While] Will Q2–8, F.
243. to] in Q2–8, F.
245. other] others Q7–8, F.
245. will] may Q2–8, F.
251. audience] answer Q2–8, F.
253. speak soon, one] speak, some one Q2–8, F.

262–263. But . . . desire] *om.* Q7–8.
263. desire] defy Q2–6, F.
264. drawest] drawl'st Q2–4, 7–8.
266. instants] an instant Q7–8.
268. An't] And Q2–8, F.
270. yet] *om.* Q3–6, F.
271. too] me Q1.
281. ventur'd] venter'd Q2–3; vent'red Q4.
282. Were great] Were as great Q5–6, F.
283. that] as Q2–8, F.
285. with] wi' Q2–6, F.
298. Whither . . . good] *om.* Q7.
299. Puff!] *om.* Q1.
300. rule] rules Q4–6.
303. their] there Q5.
305. Will . . . gone] Go, get you gone Q2–8, F.
306. word] words Q3–6, F.
306. moves] move F.
306. S.P. 1 GENTLEMAN.] 2 *Gent.* Q1.
308. they] *om.* Q2; you Q3–6, F.
308.1. *Exeunt . . . Mardonius.*] *om.* Q1.
323. chose] chosen Q8.
325. doted] done Q2–6; done it Q7–8, F.
328. venter] venture Q7–8, F.
334. good] stood Q8.
340. manifold] manifest Q7–8.
342. truth; when] truth; but when Q2–8, F.
342. of] *om.* Q2–8, F.
346. above] about Q2–8, F.
365. would shine] will shine Q3–6, F.
367. lest] jest Q3.
371. wild] *om.* Q2–8, F.
372. honest] honesty Q2–8, F.
373. would] should Q3–6, F.
374. defend] descend Q6.
375. would] should Q2–8, F.
375. out you] you out Q2–8, F.
386. thee] me Q4–6, F.
393. 'tis] it is Q2–8, F.
394. I] *om.* Q6.

398. in thine] i'thine Q2–4; in thy Q6.
404. I'those] Ith those Q1; In those Q7–8.
407. the] they Q2.
409. 'em] them Q7–8.
413. with.] with.   Enter *Bessus,* and the two *Gent.* Q2.
415. you] yon Q2.
416. 'em] them Q2–8, F.
416.1. *Enter . . . Bessus.]om.* Q1.
419. I am] I'm Q2–8, F.
420. S.P. 1 GENTLEMAN.] 2 *Gentleman.* Q2–8, F.
421. S.P. 2 GENTLEMAN.] 1 *Gentleman.* Q2–8, F.
424. you haste.] you; halfe Q1.
425. An't] And Q2–8, F.
426. Is't] Is it Q8.
428. two] to Q5.
429. Panthea] Panthan Q1; Pentha Q5–6, F.
431. be] we Q2.
432. will't] will Q1.
433. sir] *om.* Q1.
434. shalt] shall Q8.
437. and] *om.* Q1.
446.1. *Enter* Messenger] *Enter a Messenger* Q2–8, F.
446.1. *with a packet]* om. Q1–6, F.
449. Thank thee] Take that Q2–8, F.
457. Enough] I'now Q2–4; I now Q5–6; Enow Q7–8; now F.
461. here] her Q3–6, 8.
471. has hir'd] had stirr'd Q2–8, F.
475. to] in Q7–8.
478. 'em] them Q6.
482. laden] loaden Q2–8, F.
486. become] come Q5–6.
489. that] her Q1.
500. Your] Our Q5.
502. prayers] prayer Q2–8, F.
504. dangers] danger Q2–8, F.
505. saw] *om.* Q4–6.
505. S.D. *Exeunt.] om.* Q1.

[I.ii]
5. either loves] ever lov'd Q3–6, F.

9. place] plac'd F.
9. too high] too light Q1; high Q2–8, F.
16. it] *om.* Q7–8.
18. thee] *om.* Q1.
26. makes] make F.
33. have] gave Q4.
35. would] will Q2–8, F.
48.1. *Enter* Bessus.] *after l. 49* Q5–6
53. find] feel Q2–8, F.
55. requires] require F.
55. speed] haste Q2–8, F.
58. long] Lord Q2.
62. *Finis . . . Primi.]* The end of the First Act. Q2–3; *om.* Q4–8, F.

[II.i]
0.1–2. Panthea, *and waiting-women, with attendance.]* Panthæa, *and Mandane, waiting women. . . .* Q1; *Panthæa, and Mandane, waiting-women, with Attendants.* Q2–6, F; *Panthea, and Mandane, waiting-women with attendants and guards.* Q7–8.
4. know't] know it Q7–8.
17. paid] weigh'd Q2–8, F.
26. S.P. ARANE.] *Arv.* Q5; *Arb.* Q6.
31. her] *om.* Q2–8, F.
32. set] let Q1.
37. ear] ears Q5–6, F.
42. woman] mother Q2–8, F.
46. 'twill] 'twould Q2–5, 7–8, F; 'twould not Q6.
47. not] *om.* Q6.
58. mine] my Q2–8, F.
69. he] 'a Q2–6.
71. him] time Q1.
93–94. as you] *om.* Q1.
95. I am] I'm Q2–8, F.
98. prayers are] prayer is Q3–6, F.
98. I will] will I Q2–8, F.
107. S.D. *Exit* Arane.] *om.* Arane, Q1; *after* I will, *l. 105* Q3–8, F.
109. Between] Betwixt Q2–8, F.
110. We] He Q8.
115. the] *om.* Q1.
123. hear it] hear't Q2–8, F.

123. Ay] *om.* Q2–8, F.
130. near] next Q2–8, F.
131. of the] o'th' Q2–8, F.
134. whom] who F.
139. prithee] pray thee Q2–8, F.
142–143. I confess] *om.* Q1.
146. Ay] *om.* Q2–8, F.
148. whenas,] when as Q1–8, F.
148. said] say Q2–8, F.
150. when] Yet Q2–8, F.
159. 'twas so] so 'twas Q2–8; so it was F.
164. An't] And Q2–8, F.
165. nearer] near Q3–6, F.
166. Y'are] Your Q8.
167. kindnesses] kindness Q2–8, F.
168. Thalestris] Thalectris Q2–6 F.
176. she'll] she' Q8.
178. for her honesty] for honesty Q2–8, F.
178. along] a long Q2.
185. on] of Q2–7, F.
185. on her] *om.* Q8.
201. S.D. *Exit.*] *Exit Bessus.* Q2–4, 7–8; *Exit.* after l. 200 Q5–6; *om.* F.
202. S.D. *Exit*] after *too* Q1–2, 7–8; *om.* Q3–6; *Exeunt Bessus and Bacurius.* F.
203. majesty] *om.* Q8.
208. 'em] them Q6.
210. virtuous] virtues Q2–8, F.
215. or] and Q2–8, F.
217. hope] hopes F.
220. love] loves Q5–6, F.
222. my lord] *om.* Q8.
225. were] where Q5–6.
227. him] time Q1.
230. there is] there's Q3–6, F.
232. does] doth Q3–6, F.
232. his] this Q1.
237. madam] *om.* Q2–8, F.
239. S.D. *Exit* Gobrius.] after *madam?* Q2–8, F; *Exit.* after *madam?* Q1.
243. S.D. *Exeunt women.*] *om.* Q1.
255. the] a Q6.
256. talk] take Q1–8, F.
263. foul] fool Q6.

268. Prithee] pray thee Q2–8, F.
270. shape] sharp Q6.
281. own] one Q5–6.
281. too] so Q2–8, F.
291. those] these Q3–6, F.
296. shall] will Q3–6, F.
305. You] Your Q4–5.
305. Thalestris] Thalectris Q2–6.
307. my] *om.* Q1.
308. others] other Q4–6, F.
315. S.D. *Exeunt.*] *Exit.* Q1.

[II.ii]
1. run] *om.* Q8.
3. women out] out women Q3–6, F.
3. fiddling] sidling Q5.
6. say] said Q2–8, F.
12. look] looks Q6.
12. those] these Q5–6, F.
14. quickly] *om.* Q2–8, F.
15. afoot] a foot Q6; o' foot F.
18. look'd] looke Q1.
20.1. *Enter . . . Philip.*] *Enter a man with two Citizens wives.* Q2–8, F.
27. S.P. 2] 3. Q5–6.
30. with me down] down with me Q3–6, F.
31. abed] to bed Q2–8, F.
32. 'tis] it is Q2–8, F.
33. prithee] pray thee Q2–8, F.
39. i'th'] 'the Q2.
42. S.P. 2] 1. Q3.
44. In] I' Q2–8, F.
45–46. Philip . . . place.] *Indented as though a separate speech with* Philip *as speech prefix* Q2–3.
49. S.P. 3 MAN.] 1. Q1.
50. you] *om.* Q1.
50. thrust] trust Q6.
52. shroving] thrusting Q1; showing Q2–6, F; shoving Q7–8.
53. hap to] haps Q2–8, F.
55. so] *om.* Q2–8, F.
59. have] ha' Q2–8, F.
63. struck] stroke Q4–6.
64. law] la Q2–8, F.
64. thou art] thou'rt Q2–8, F.
64. there is] there's Q2–8, F.

65. thou art] thou'rt Q2–8, F.
65. one] one one Q3.
65. of it] on't Q2–8, F.
66. he will] he'll Q2–8, F.
67. slipstring] stripling Q1.
70. S.P. 3 MAN.] *om.* Q6.
71. you are] you're Q2–8, F.
72. cost] cast Q2–6.
72. fall.] fall./ *Flourish. Enter one running.* Q2–5, 7–8, F; . . . *owne running.* Q6.
73. S.P. 3 MAN.] 4. Q2–8, F.
74.1. *Enter . . . others.*] *Flourish. Enter Arbaces, Tigranes, the two Kings, and Mardonius.* Q2–8, F.
76. thank] think Q5–6.
85. without] but with Q2–8, F.
85. our] your Q3–6, F.
87. in] i' Q2–6, F.
88. you may] may Q5–6, F.
93. may you] you may Q3–6, F.
93. all] fall Q6.
94. when] where Q3–6, F.
99. Behold] Beheld Q5–6.
99. hearts] heart Q2–8, F.
103. S.P. WOMAN.] *3 Woman.* Q1–8, F.
103. hang him] *om.* Q2–6, F.
106. was far] was so far Q3–6, F.
109. Not] Nor Q5–6.
110. nature] name F.
114. with] *om.* Q7–8.
114. and won] and I won Q7–8.
115. brought] made Q1.
118. will] well Q3–4.
119. work] word Q3–6.
121. commendations] commendation Q2–8, F.
126. Thus] That Q2–8, F.
127. calls] call Q2–8, F.
128. amongst] among Q4–6, F.
133. Eat] Sit Q2–8, F.
135. to] so Q4.
137. God . . . majesty!] *om.* Q1.
137.1. *Exeunt . . . train.*] *Exeunt.* after *all,* 1. 136 Q1; *Flourish. Exeunt kings and their train.* after *all* l. 136 Q2–8, F.

139. God's] God Q5–6, F.
142. haltersack] holtersack Q6.
143. S.P. 2 MAN.] 1. Q1.
146. so] *om.* Q1.
147–148. S.D. *Exeunt . . . Woman.*] *Exeunt* 1, 2, 3, *and Women.* Q1; *Exeunt* 2, 3. *and Women.* Q2–4, 7–8; . . ./ 2. 3. *and woman.* Q5–6, F (*all after l. 146*).
148. afore] before F.
148. h o m e w a r d] h o m e w a r d s Q2–8, F.
149. all] *om.* Q1.
152. They are] They're Q2–8, F.
152. on] of F.
157. *Finis . . . Secundi.*] The end of the Second Act. Q2–3; *om.* Q4–8, F.

[III.i]
1. take] takes Q6.
2. doth] does Q2–5, 7–8, F.
9. will] would Q5–6, F.
15. I do . . . not] *om.* Q1.
22. Sir, she'll] She will Q2–8, F.
30. For] fore Q5.
31. would] could Q3–6, F.
34. you] *om.* Q3–6.
38.1. 1 Gentleman *and*] *om.* Q1.
39. *and* 40. S.P. 1 GENTLEMAN.] *Gent.* Q1.
39. here's] here is Q2–8, F.
41. them] 'em Q2–8, F.
44.2. 2 Gentleman, *and* Bessus.] *and Bessus* Q1; *and Bessus, and two Gentlemen.* Q2–6, F; *and Bessus, and two Gentlemen, Attendants, and Guards.* Q7–8.
46. is] to Q1.
55. sorrow] sorrows Q3–6, F.
58. S.P. ARBACES.] *Ara.* Q2–6.
59. guard] guide Q2–8, F.
59. S.D. *Exit Arane.*] *Exit.* Q1 (*after still l. 58*).
77. kindness] kind ones Q7–8.
80. thyself] myself Q4.
82. thence] hence Q2–6, F.
82. there] here Q7–8.
84. flesh] breast Q2–8, F.

85. a] thy Q3–6, F.
86. wanton] wonted Q4–6, F.
87. in thy] i' thy Q2–8, F.
100. that may] that it may Q3–6, F.
101. manhood] manhood's Q8.
118–122. ARBACES. Your. . . .
Where?]*Arb.* Your . . . sir?/ *Gob.*
Someone . . . she?/ *Arb.* Do . . .
there?/ *Gob.* Where?/ *Arb.*
There./ *Gob.* There? Where? Q1.
118. has] hath Q2–8, F.
119. where] *om.* Q8.
132. But] And Q2–8, F.
137. sleep] sheep Q2–8, F.
145. yet] *om.* Q2–8, F.
150–152. She . . . thus.] *om.* Q1.
154. hold] holp Q8.
166. any] ever Q2–8, F.
174. is she] she is Q3–6, F.
192. your] my Q3–6, F.
199. them] 'em Q2–8, F.
201. so] see Q2–8, F.
209. change] rage Q2–8, F.
211. God] heaven Q3–6, F.
222. in the] i'th' Q2–8, F.
224. one] own Q6.
237. how dare you then] how then
dare you Q3–4; then how dare you
Q5–6, F.
239. do] *om.* Q8.
244. that] the Q3–6, F.
247. law] laws Q2–8, F.
270. fam'd] fram'd Q3–6.
270. tyrant's] Titan's Q3–6, F.
271. in the] i'the Q2–8, F.
271. depth] deep Q3–8, F.
274.1. *Exeunt . . . Bacurius.*] *om.*
Q1; *Exit . . .* Q2–8, F.
285. was] *om.* Q8.
293. too. . . . Here] to hear
Q3–6, F.
302. do I] I do Q2–8, F.
304. still] yet Q2–8, F.
305. This, this third] This third
Q2–6, 8, F.
310. S.P. GOBRIUS.] *Panthea.* Q1.
315. poisoner] prisoner Q4–6, F.
316. GOBRIUS. Madam. . . . PAN-

THEA. Nay] *Bac.* Madam. . . ./
Gob. Nay Q1.
322. had it] had 't Q2–8, F.
322. 'twixt] betwixt Q2–8, F.
323.1. *Exeunt . . . Mardonius.*]
*Exeunt Gobrius, Panthea, Bessus,
and Spaconia.* Q3–6, F; *Exeunt
Gobrius, Panthea, and Bessus.*
Q7–8.
337. prithee] pray thee Q2–8, F.
338. I not] not I Q2, 7–8.
343. no] do Q6.
344. ye] you Q2–8, F.
347. prithee] pray thee Q2–8, F.
349. MARDONIUS. . . . ye.] *om.*
Q2–8, F.

[III.ii]
0.1. *Enter* Bessus.] *Enter Bessus
alone.* Q2–8, F.
1. fame] game Q7–8.
3. have it but] have but Q2, 7–8.
13. on] o— Q3.
15. them] 'em Q2–8, F.
15. In this] I' this Q2–4, 7–8; Ay,
this Q5–6, F.
16. by th'] b' the Q2–6.
16. with] wi' Q2–5, 7–8, F.
17. would have] would ha' Q7–8.
18. with] wi' Q2–5, 7–8, F.
22. God] heaven Q3–6, F.
22. call'd] calls Q5–6, F.
23. pounds] pound Q2–8, F.
30. afraid] 'fraid Q2–6, F.
37. of] on Q2–8, F.
38. to account] *om.* Q2–8, F.
38. the] *om.* Q2, 7–8.
39.1. a] *om.* Q1.
40. S.P. GENTLEMAN.] *3 Gentleman.*
in all speech prefixes to exit at
l. 80 Q2–8, F.
43. You are] You're Q2–8, F.
46. nothing doubts] doth nothing
doubt Q2–8, F.
50. it is] 'tis Q7–8.
55. cry you] cir you Q5; sir,
your F.
56. agreeably] agreeable Q4–6, 8, F.

58. Um, um, um . . . um, um, um]
Um . . . um Q1 (*and so throughout speech*).
59. an] *om.* Q2–8, F.
65. can] could Q2–8, F.
66. S.P. BESSUS.] om. Q1.
73. with you] *om.* Q2–8, F.
74. do] show Q2–8, F.
75. resolutely] resolvedly Q2–8, F.
75. hundred] hundreth Q2–3.
77. ye] you Q2–8, F.
80. S.D. *Exit* Gentleman.] *Exit*:
Q1; *Exit* 3. *Gen*: Q2–8, F (*all after
l. 79*).
83. this] these Q4.
85. by] my Q8.
86. so] so that Q2–7, F.
86. reserv'd] referr'd Q2–8, F.
88. these] there Q1.
89. likely] like Q2–8, F.
89. this] these Q4.
90. five year] time here Q1.
90. year] years Q4–6, 8, F.
91. send] find Q2–8, F.
98. 'em] them Q6.
112. own] one Q5–6.
122. prithee] pray thee Q2–8, F.
123. beat] beaten Q5–6, F.
125. pounds] pound Q2–8, F.
126. leg well a week] leg a week
Q1; leg well a waeke Q5; leg well
and walk Q6.
133. a] *om.* Q4–6.
137. you wear] your were Q3.
138. quick] *om.* F.
145. very] *om.* Q7–8.
151. S.D. *Exit.*] *Exit Bacurius.*
Q2–8, F.
154. beating] beting Q5–6.
158–159. will I] I will Q2–8, F.
159. all is] all that's Q2–6, F; all
that is Q7–8.
160. S.D. *Exit.*] *Exit Bessus.*
Q2–8, F.

[III.iii]
1. He is] He's Q7–8.
5. await] wait Q3–6, F.
8. S.D. *Enter* Arbaces.] *after* again,

l. 7 Q2–8, F; *om.* Q1.
11. in their] i' their Q2–8, F.
14. lies] lie F.
16. me] 'em F.
19. do] *om.* Q1.
23. Are] Art Q1.
24. not that] it not Q3–6, F.
24. there's] there is Q7–8.
28. shall not shrink] will not
shrink Q3–6, F.
29. you] your Q6.
30. 'tis] it is F.
31. hath] has Q2–8, F.
31. were] wear Q6.
32. a fall] fall Q1.
32. fall, or, sleeping] fall, sleeping Q6.
42. all] *om.* Q2–8, F.
48. Shall I] I shall Q3–6, F.
51. what] *om.* Q2–8, F.
52. should] shall Q3–6, F.
56. on] one Q3–6, F.
62. a] *om.* Q1.
63. There is] There's Q6.
65. do it] do't Q6.
68. I do] you do Q3–6, F.
87. cause] case Q3–6, F.
88. how] ha how Q4–6, F.
90. about] upon Q4–6, F.
91. his] this Q3–6, F.
92. Dear] Hear Q2–8, F.
95. Pray God] Heaven grant
Q3–6, F.
107. no] nor Q6.
108. God] the gods Q3–4, F; thee
gods Q5–6.
108. mend you] mend Q3–6, F.
110. require] requires Q3–6, F.
114. of] for Q3–6, F.
115.1. *to them*] *om.* Q2–8, F.
116. Where is] Where's Q2, 7–8.
121. Away] A way Q5.
123. I am] I'm Q2–8, F.
125–127. well. . . ./ MARDONIUS. If]
well./ *Mar.* I . . . . If Q1.
126. I am] I'm Q3–5, F.
127. that] this Q3–6, F.
129–131. BESSUS. . . . you.] *om.* Q1.

133. occasions] occasion Q3–6, F.
137. the] these Q4–6, F.
138. his] this Q5–6, F.
138. S.D. *Exit.*] *Exit Mardonius.*
Q2–8, F.
140. Do't] Doe Q1.
140. without] out Q3.
144. a] the Q4–6, F.
147. would have] would fain have
Q7–8.
148. understand'st] understands
Q1.
149. a bout] about Q1–6.
151. Dost make] Dost thou make
Q2–8, F.
152–153. be, tell me] b me Q3; be
Q4–6, F.
153. too] *om.* Q1.
156. and] thou Q4–8, F.
159–160. ever you] ever your Q2.
163. have] *om.* Q5–6, F.
164. Like flames] Like the flames
Q3–6, F.
169. your] my Q4–6, F.
173. horror. I] horror. Now I
Q3–8, F.
188. God's . . . man's] God . . .
man Q7–8, F.
189. nature's] nature Q7–8.
192. S.D. *Exit* Bessus.] *after sin*
Q1–8, F.
196. *Finis Actus Tertii.*] The end
of the Third Act. Q2–3; *om.*
Q4–8, F.

[IV.i]
0.1. Panthea, Spaconia] Panthea,
and Spaconia F.
8. since] *om.* Q4–6, F.
8. th'are] they are Q2–8, F.
10. 'em] them Q6.
11. 'em] them Q6.
12. Though] If Q1.
15. out] on't Q2–8, F.
16. against] 'gainst Q2–8, F.
23. shoot] shot Q4–6.
27. not] no Q6.
27. further] farther Q2–8, F.
29. But] *om.* Q1.

38. S.D. *Exit* Gobrius.] *Exit.* Q1
(*after* brother, *l.* 37).
45. yours] you Q2–8, F.
55. S.P. PANTHEA.] *Spaconia.* Q2.
59. I am] I'm Q7–8.
59. not] no Q1.
66. those] these Q2–8.
67. tame] have Q1.
68. beside] besides Q6.
71. word] words Q1.
73. I'm] I am Q2–8, F.
80. God] Heaven Q3–6, F.

[IV.ii]
0.1. *Enter* Tigranes.] *Enter Tigranes in prison.* Q2–8, F.
2. mine] my Q2–5, 7–8, F.
2. turn'd] turne Q1.
14. it] *om.* Q3–6, F.
20. griefs] grief Q2–8, F.
22. woman's] women Q2–5, 7–8, F;
woman Q6.
23. lost] left Q2–8, F.
26. inconstancy] unconstancy Q7–8.
33–34. me. . . . Lady,/ Your]
Ladie./ *Enter Bac. and Spac./
Bac.* Your Q1.
39. for] or Q2–8, F.
44. the] your Q2–8, F.
50. as firm] is firm Q3–6, F.
51. and] *om.* Q2–8, F.
52. in the air] in th'air Q3; i'th'
air Q4–6, F.
55. murmurs] murmur Q2–8, F.
61. wrongs] wrong Q5–6, F.
64. S.P. SPACONIA.] *om.* Q1.
65. alike] *om.* Q4–6, F.
70. beshrew] beshrow Q5–8, F.
72. He's] 'tis Q2–8, F.
74. spoken] spoke Q8.
80. me] *om.* Q2–8, F.
82. No] Nay Q3–6, F.
82.1. *and*] *om.* Q2–8, F.
85. quit] quite Q2–4, 7–8.
94. outlast two] last too F.
99. lady is] lady's Q2–8, F.
105. know] knew Q2–8, F.
110. prattling] prating Q2–8, F.
111. to it] to't Q2–8, F.

114. bar] bare Q6.
115. Beside] Besides F.
117. Sirrah] Sir Q2–8, F.
122. pok'd] yok'd Q2–8, F.
123. broke] broken Q5–6, F.
124. trifled] stifled Q4–6.
134. say, sir, what you please] say what you please, sir Q2–8, F.
135. S.P. MARDONIUS.] om. Q2–8, F.
142. God] heaven Q3–6, F.
144. do it] do't Q2–8, F.
145. Do] om. Q1.
152–153. and . . . Termagant] om. Q2–8, F.
155. let 'em] let them Q2–8, F.
155. be prisoners] prisoners be Q2–8, F.
157. 'em] them Q6.
158. S.P. BACURIUS.] Tigranes. Q2–8, F.
159. S.P. SPACONIA.] om. Q2–6, F.
160. dear] dearer Q4–6, F.
160.1. Exit . . . Spaconia.] Exeunt Tigranes, Spaconia, Bacurius. Q2–8, F.
161. have you] you have Q4–6, F.
162. reprove] prove Q6.
165. saddler's] sutler's Q2–8, F.
166. to] no Q5.
169. wonnot] will not Q7–8.
172. then] om. Q2–8, F.
172. these] this Q2.
175. Where] When Q2–8, F.
175. 'em] them Q6.
176. Do . . . me] om. Q2–8, F.
177. grow] grow worse Q2–8, F.
178. rock'd] rott Q1–8, F.
179. dead] deep Q4–6, F.
180. Till] Like Q1.
185. all] om. Q2–8, F.
187. Wo't] Wilt Q7–8.
187. my] good Q1.
193. all] om. Q3–6, F.
196. do] to Q2–8, F.
199. tame] have Q1.
202. heart] heat Q5–6.
203. her] here Q5.
203. a] om. Q5–6.

207. Prithee] Pray thee Q2–8, F.
211. knew of] knew'st Q2–4, 7–8; know'st Q5–6, F.
220. is it] it is Q2–8, F.
228. be thousand] be a thousand Q6, F.
229. Thousands] om. Q1; Thousand Q5–6.
229. deny it] deny't Q2–7, F.
231. where] were Q8.
231. virtue] virtues Q3–6, F.
236. S.D. Exeunt.] Exeunt all. Q2–8, F.

[IV.iii]
5. understood] understand Q2–8, F.
7. my] om. Q3–6, F.
8. to the] to th' Q2–3, 7–8.
10. 2 SWORDMAN. . . . honor.] om. Q6.
11–12. cause . . . truth./ BESSUS. My] cause./ Bessus. Be . . . my Q2–8, F.
17. have] has Q2–8, F.
18. he] 'a Q2–5; I Q6.
24. case] cause Q2–8, F.
25. honorable] horrible Q3–6, F.
27. we] the Q3–6, F.
30. drawn ten] drawen Q3; drawn Q4–6, F.
30. beside] besides F.
31. these] this Q2–8, F.
31. had] bad Q4.
34. he] 'a Q2–5.
35. crossing] tossing Q2–8, F.
38. gentlemen] gentleman Q1.
39. There's] There is F.
46. mile] miles Q4–6, F.
47. err] ere Q5.
47. mile] miles F.
49–53. BESSUS. 'Tis . . . sword.] Bes. Tis . . . must/ Be . . . vertuous./ 1. Obedience . . . ont,/ To . . . bodie;/ I . . . sword. Q1.
49. o'the] the Q4–6, F.
61. sword] swrod Q5; word Q6.
61. lost . . . forc'd] forc'd . . . lost Q1–8, F.

64. case] cause Q5–6, F.
66. sit] set Q2–6, F; sat Q7–8.
67. it had] 't had Q2–8, F.
69. delivering] delivery Q5–6.
73. He] 'A Q2–5; And Q6.
73. delivery] delivering Q5–6, F.
77. th'] the Q2–8, F.
78. You are] You're Q2–8, F.
81. the] *om.* Q1.
85. what] that Q2, 7–8.
86. sir] sirs Q2–8, F.
86. th'] the Q2–8, F.
87. kick'd, captain] kick'd, the captain Q6.
88. he's] is Q2–8, F.
89. But . . . brother?] *om.* Q2–8, F.
93. Surely] Surly Q5–6.
94. You] Your Q5; You'll Q6.
96. This] The Q2–8, F.
99. the] this Q2–8, F.
101. Give] I Give Q5–6; Ay, give F.
101. Again!] *om.* Q2–8, F.
101. Brother] *om.* Q6.
102. I] *om.* Q5.
106. And my fox] and fox Q6.
106. "Musted"] musled Q1.
109. untemperate] intemperate Q4–6, F.
112. kicker] kicke Q1.
114. beaten] baren Q6.
114. may] will Q6.
115. error?] error I Q6.
118. one] on Q5–6.
122. foot] foole Q1.
122. A] Ah Q1.
123. mighty] weighty Q6.
124. laugh'd] laugh Q4–6, F.
126. S.P. 2 SWORDMAN.] 1. Q1.
136. size] sizes Q6.
147. abide upon't] bide upon Q2–8, F.
150. Boy] Both Q6.
150. get some] get me some Q4–6, F.
151. clear] clean Q6.
152. when] *om.* Q2–8, F.
153. We] you Q7–8.
158. S.P. 2] *3* Q6.

158. We] Go Q6.
159. be] are Q5–6, F.

[IV.iv]
0.1. *door,* Gobrius] *door, and Gobrius* Q2–8, F.
3. S.D. *Exit* Gobrius.] *om.* Q1.
4. You are] You're Q2–8, F.
4. I] *om.* Q4–6, F.
4. God] heaven Q3–6, F.
8. these] the Q7–8.
9. should] shall Q2–3, 6–8.
9. speak?] speak I Q6.
11. does] doth Q2–8, F.
12. brought'st] broughts Q1.
13. heard] head Q6.
14. prithee] pray thee Q2–8, F.
15. I am] Am I Q3–6.
15. the] she Q5.
28. As] *om.* Q3–6, F.
32. prithee] pray thee Q2–5, 7–8, F; pray the Q6.
37. that there is a cause] and there is a cause Q3–4; and there is no cause Q5; and there is none can see Q6.
45. prison] prisoner Q6.
50. step] stop Q4–6.
55. God] Heaven Q3–6, F.
56. cause] case F.
63. innocents] innocence Q2–8, F.
64. Know I] Know that I Q3–6, F.
65. beast] best Q6.
66. it is] 'tis Q3–6, F.
69. as] where Q3–6, F.
78. God] heaven Q3–6, F.
81. e'en] eye Q1.
84. 'em] them Q6.
86. Far] Fare Q5.
87. should] shall Q2–8, F.
93. 'em] them Q6.
100. though thou wert] though tho' wert Q2–3, 7.
102. sins] sin Q3–6, F.
112. stop] steppe Q1.
114. else] elfe Q5.
119. 'em] them Q6.
120. them] 'em Q2–8, F.
122. 'em] them Q6.

123. raze] raise Q6.
123. 'em . . . 'em] them . . . them Q6.
123. then] them F.
124. 'em] them Q6.
124. them] 'em Q2–8, F.
126. 'em] them Q6.
140–141. I . . . was./ ARBACES. Stay . . . births] *Arbaces.* I . . . was,/ Stay . . . births Q2–8, F.
144. in this] i'this Q2.
145. there's] there is Q2–8, F.
147. Why] *om.* Q1.
150. I know] *om.* Q3–6, F.
155. were scrupulous] were too scrupulous Q3–6, F.
159–160. I . . . yours] I dare no longer stay Q7–8.
160. I fear] *om.* Q3–6, F.
162. God's] heaven's Q3–6, F.
163. S.D. *Exeunt.*] *om.* Q1; *Exeunt several ways.* Q3–6, F.
164. *Finis Actus Quarti.*] The end of the Fourth Act. Q2–3; *om.* Q4–8, F.

[V.i]
2. leave] power Q2–8, F.
4. hands] hand Q2–8, F.
9. offices] Officers Q1.
24. he] 'a Q2–6.
27. something] so much Q2–8, F.
32. the] *om.* Q2–8, F.
41. had] *om.* Q8.
49. h'as] he has Q5–6, F.
51. he] 'a Q2–6.
52. in his] in's Q2–5, 7–8, F; in in's Q6.
54. o'] in Q6; i' Q7–8.
56. to] two Q3–6, F.
59–60. He/ Is] Is Q1; He's Q7–8.
60. low] base Q2–8, F.
61. should] shall Q2–8, F.
63. strange] *om.* Q3–6, F.
68. broke] broken Q5–6, F.
69. of] on Q2–8, F.
74. S.D. *Exit.*] *Exit Mardonius.* Q1–8, F.
74.1. *and* Swordmen] *and the*

Swordmen Q2–8, F.
82. kick you, and thus] kick, and thus Q2–8; kick, thus F.
86. 'a] he Q7–8, F.
89. a] an Q4–6, F.
89. S.D. *again*] *om.* Q3–8, F.
92–94. LIGONES. Sir . . . attempt] *Lig.* Sir . . . lie/ With . . . Sir./ *Bes.* My . . . attempt Q1.
92. Sir] *om.* Q3–6, F.
98. your] your your Q2.
108. your] you Q2–8, F.
110. would] will Q3–6, F.
111. Now] Not Q4–5, F.
117. sensible] sensibly Q7–8.
118. of] from Q3–6, F.
121. pray'ee] pray Q2–8, F.
121. S.D. *Exit* Ligones.] *after* captain, *l. 120* Q1–8, F. (*om.* Ligones Q1)
125. honor's] honor Q2–8, F.
127. A'] Have Q2–8, F.
127. S.P. BESSUS.] *om.* Q1.
128. S.P. 2 SWORDMAN.] *om.* F.
129. he . . . he] 'a . . . 'a Q2–6.
131. S.D. *Exeunt.*] *Exeunt clear.* Q2–6, F; *Exeunt omnes.* Q7–8.

[V.ii]
4.1. *Enter . . . Spaconia.*] *after* indeed, *l. 5* Q1.
11. business] businesses Q4–6, F.
14. Armenian] Armenia Q2.
32–33. commendation] commendations Q2–6.
34. would] that Q3–6, F.
38. mine] my Q2–5, 7–8, F.
42. and like] and I like Q2–8, F.
46. in the] i'the Q2–8, F.
49. any] my Q2.
51. enough] enow Q3–6, F.
51. beside] besides Q2–8, F.
55. men] man Q2–8, F.
57. corns] comes Q4.
58. your] a Q2–8, F.
65. should] shall Q2–8, F.
68. Arbaces] Arbcus Q5–6.
72. a] *om.* Q2–8, F.
77. God] heaven Q3–6, F.

80. in my] in all my Q3–6, F.
83. S.D. *Exit.*] *Exit Ligones.* Q2–8, F.
89. shall] should Q2–8, F.
91. S.D. *Exeunt.*] *Exeunt all.* Q2–8, F.

[V.iii]
0.1. *a*] *his* Q3–8, F.
2.1. *Enter . . . Swordmen.*] *Enter Bessus with the two Swordmen.* after *in*, l. 2 Q2–8, F.
7. is mistaken] is much mistaken Q5–6, F.
9. can] *om.* Q2–8, F.
12. a] *om.* Q1.
12. lancing] laming Q2–8, F.
13. fall] full Q1.
18. I confess] I must confess Q2–8, F.
21. God] heaven Q3–6, F.
22. come] tome Q5; to me Q6.
31. most] more Q8.
34. S.P. BACURIUS.] *om.* Q1.
34. S.P. 1 SWORDMAN.] *Swordman.* Q6.
40. think] think on F.
41. They] That Q6.
47. here] there Q2–8, F.
51. their] the Q2–8, F.
55. Ye . . . . Ye] You . . . . You Q2–8, F.
57. You] Your Q1–8, F.
59. many] bevy Q2–5, 7–8, F; beauty Q6.
61. do] do do Q5.
63. S.P. 1] *2* Q8.
71. slave? My key] slave? My toe Q2, 7–8; hurts my toe Q3–6, F.
72. with't] with it Q2–8, F.
78. nothing] anything F.
79.1. *Enter* Servant.] *om.* Q1; *Enter Servant, Will. Adkinson:* Q2.
80. Here's] Here is Q5–6, F.
81. I am] I'm Q2–8, F.
81. prithee] pray thee Q2–8, F.
81. 'em] them Q2–8, F.
83. but men] but men, sir Q2–8, F.
84. bones. . . . Up with] bones;

captain, rally up Q2–5, 7–8, F; bones; captain, rally upon Q6.
86. hold] ho Q2–8, F.
89. breath] health Q3–6, F.
89. S.D. *Exit* Bacurius.] *om.* Q1.
91. I'm] I am Q2–8, F.
91. ha'] have Q2–8, F.
92. he . . . he] 'a . . . 'a Q2–6.
93. besides] beside Q3–6.
95. God] heaven Q3–6, F.
96. he has] h'as Q2–8, F.
98. is] and Q4–6, F.
100. hands] hand Q2–8, F.
104. shoes] shows Q5–6.
104.1. *Exeunt.*] *Exeunt clear.* Q2–6, F; *Exeunt omnes.* Q7–8.

[V.iv]
1. bore] bare Q5–6, F.
2–7. Hell . . . mine] *om.* Q2–8, F.
8. friend] friends Q5–6, F.
9. an] that Q3–6, F.
15. he] 'a Q2–6.
16. does . . . hand] do . . . hands F.
20–21. I . . . mark'd–] *Mar.* I . . . . Begone./ Sir . . . mark'd– Q1.
24. humblier] humbler Q2–8, F.
42. do. I] do, and I Q3–6, F.
51. toys] tales Q7–8.
55. should] would Q5–6, F.
58. Far-] For Q2–8, F.
60. God] Heaven Q3–6, F.
60. temperate] temporal Q2, 7.
61. S.D. *Exit* Mardonius.] *after* fear Q1–2, 7–8 (*om.* Mardonius Q1); *om.* F.
62. errors] error Q5–6, F.
68. Curses incurable] Curses more incurable Q3–6, F.
76. for pay] for my pay Q5–6, F.
93. And when] and I when Q1.
94–95. in/To] into Q1, 5–6, F.
98. meant'st] mean'st Q2, 6.
98. a] to Q4–6, F.
99. God] heaven Q3–6, F.
103. wouldst] shouldst Q3–6, F.
110. into] in to Q4.
115. to yourself] thyself Q2–8, F.
119. know it] know't Q2–6, F.

129. wrung] wrong Q5–6.
140. thou] thy Q5–6, F.
141. S.D. *Draws . . . sword.*] *om.* Q1–7, F; *after* me Q8.
158. expect'st] expects Q1, 3; **ex-**pectes Q2.
163. Thou] Then Q2–8, F.
175. a] *om.* Q4–6, F.
181. you] *om.* Q1.
182. S.P. ARBACES.] *Arane.* Q2–4.
183. hear] here Q2–3.
188. as she] thought she was F.
207. opportunity] opportunities Q2–8, F.
211. God was humbly thank'd] humble thanks was given Q3–6, F.
212. That . . . queen] *om.* Q3–6, F.
219. least] lest Q2.
222. Quick] Quickly Q5–6, F.
223. abed] to bed Q2–8, F.
227. sware] swore Q2–8, F.
232. the] this Q2–8, F.
236. year] years F.
244. talk] tale Q2–8, F.
249. spark] sparks Q2–8, F.
252. am] be Q3–6, F.
253. are] be Q2–8, F.
254. too] *om.* Q1.
255. God] heaven Q3–6, F.
257. S.P. GOBRIUS.] *om.* Q1.
258. who] wo Q6.
258. dare] dares Q2–8, F.
259. them] 'em Q2–8, F.
260. wait'st] waites Q1–2; **waits** Q3–8; wait F.
262. S.D. *Enter . . . others.*] *after* welcome Q1; *Enter Bessus, Gentlemen, Mardonius, and other Attendants. after welcome,* Q2–8, F.
263. Mardonius] *Mardonius. (as*

speech prefix) Q2; *om.* Q3–8, F.
265. so] *om.* Q1.
265. happiest] happy Q5–6.
268. One] On, Q1.
271. house] home Q6.
271. S.D. *Exit* 1 Gentleman.] *om.* Q1; *Exit a Gentleman. after of,* l. 273 Q2–8, F.
277–278. I . . . be./ Nay . . . me;] *om.* Q1.
282. but] *om.* Q2–8, F.
284. here] her Q6.
294. I said] I say Q1; I, and Q2–8, F.
299. he's] he is Q2–8, F.
300. state] king Q1.
301. Ligones] Lignes Q6.
309. S.D. *Exit* 2 Gentleman.] *om.* Q1; *Exit two Gent.* Q2–6, F; *Exeunt two Gent.* Q7–8.
316. He] 'A Q2; An Q3; One Q4–6, F.
317. shall] shalt F, Q8.
319. That] *om.* Q6.
323. thing] thinke Q1.
326. S.D. *Enter . . . Gentleman.*] *after* you, l. 328 Q2–8, F; *Enter Pan. after* queen!— Q1.
334. S.D. *Enter . . . Gentleman.*] *om.* Q1–8, F.
334. S.P. BACURIUS.] *Mar.* Q1; 2 *Gent.* Q2–8, F.
335. at first] *om.* Q1.
337. S.D. *Enter . . . Spaconia.*] *after* queen, l. 336 Q1; *after* more, l. 336 Q2–8, F.
347. 'em] them Q6.
349. And you] and your Q1–8.
354. FINIS.] *om.* F.

Appendix B

Chronology

Because of their large number and of difficulties in dating, an incomplete list of the "Beaumont and Fletcher" plays is given. Dates are those assigned by E. K. Chambers, *The Elizabethan Stage*, and G. E. Bentley, *The Jacobean and Caroline Stage;* ascriptions of authorship are those of C. H. Hoy, *Studies in Bibliography*, Vols. VIII–XV. Approximate years are indicated by *, occurrences in doubt by (?).

Political and Literary Events	*Life and Works of Beaumont and Fletcher*
1579	
John Lyly's *Euphues: The Anatomy of Wit* published.	John Fletcher born at Rye, Sussex.
Sir Thomas North's translation of Plutarch's *Lives*.	
1580	
Thomas Middleton born.	
1583	
Philip Massinger born.	Sir John Beaumont, brother of Francis, born.
1584	
Raleigh sends Amadas and Barlow to Virginia.	Francis Beaumont born at Grace-Dieu, Leicestershire.*
1586	
Death of Sir Philip Sidney.	
John Ford born.	
1587	
Drake raids Cadiz.	
The Rose theater opened by Henslowe.	
Execution of Mary, Queen of Scots.	
Marlowe's *TAMBURLAINE*, Part I.*	

1588
Defeat of the Spanish Armada.
Marlowe's *TAMBURLAINE,*
Part II.*

1589
Marlowe's *JEW OF MALTA.*
Kyd's *SPANISH TRAGEDY.*
Greene's *FRIAR BACON AND
FRIAR BUNGAY.*

1590
Spenser's *Faerie Queene* (Books
I–III) published.
Sidney's *Arcadia* published.
Shakespeare's *HENRY VI,* Parts
I–III,* *TITUS ANDRONICUS.*

1591
Shakespeare's *RICHARD III.*   Fletcher admitted a pensioner of
Bene't (Corpus Christi) College,
Cambridge (?).

1592
Marlowe's *DOCTOR FAUSTUS,*
EDWARD II.
Shakespeare's *TAMING OF THE
SHREW,* *COMEDY OF ER-
RORS.*
Death of Greene.

1593
Shakespeare's *LOVE'S LABOR'S
LOST;* *Venus and Adonis* pub-
lished.
Death of Marlowe.
Theaters closed on account of
plague.

1594
Shakespeare's *TWO GENTLE-*   Fletcher takes Cambridge B.A. (?)
MEN OF VERONA; *The Rape
of Lucrece* published.
Shakespeare's company becomes
Lord Chamberlain's Men.
James Shirley born.*
Death of Kyd.

1595

The Swan theater built.

Sidney's *Defense of Poesy* published.

Shakespeare's *ROMEO AND JULIET,* MIDSUMMER NIGHT'S DREAM,* RICHARD II.**

Raleigh's first expedition to Guiana.

1596

Spenser's *Faerie Queene* (Books IV–VI) published.

Shakespeare's *MERCHANT OF VENICE,* KING JOHN.**

Beaumont matriculates at Broadgates Hall (later Pembroke), Oxford, February 4.

Fletcher's father, Bishop of London, dies in straitened circumstances.

1597

Bacon's *Essays* (first edition).

Shakespeare's *HENRY IV*, Part I.*

1598

Demolition of the Theatre.

Shakespeare's *MUCH ADO ABOUT NOTHING,* HENRY IV*, Part II.*

Jonson's *EVERY MAN IN HIS HUMOR* (first version).

Seven books of Chapman's translation of Homer's *Iliad* published.

With brothers John and Henry, Beaumont leaves Oxford upon death of his father.

Fletcher takes Cambridge M.A. (?).

1599

Globe theater opened.

Shakespeare's *AS YOU LIKE IT,* HENRY V,* JULIUS CAESAR.**

Dekker's *SHOEMAKERS' HOLIDAY.**

Death of Spenser.

1600

Shakespeare's *TWELFTH NIGHT,* HAMLET.**

Marston's *ANTONIO AND MELLIDA,* ANTONIO'S REVENGE.**

Beaumont enters Inner Temple, November 3.

The Fortune theater built by
Alleyn.

1601
Shakespeare's *MERRY WIVES OF
WINDSOR.**
Insurrection and execution of the
Earl of Essex.

1602
Shakespeare's *TROILUS AND
CRESSIDA,** *ALL'S WELL THAT
ENDS WELL.**

Beaumont's first verse published—
a commendatory poem prefixed to
Sir John Beaumont's *Metamor-
phosis of Tobacco*. Followed by
Salmacis and Hermaphroditus.

1603
Death of Queen Elizabeth; acces-
sion of James VI of Scotland as
James I.
Shakespeare's company becomes
the King's Men.
Florio's translation of Montaigne's
Essays published.
Heywood's *WOMAN KILLED
WITH KINDNESS.*
Marston's *THE MALCONTENT.**

1604
Shakespeare's *MEASURE FOR
MEASURE,** *OTHELLO.**
Marston's *FAWN.**
Chapman's *BUSSY D'AMBOIS.**

1605
Shakespeare's *KING LEAR.**
Marston's *DUTCH COURTE-
ZAN.**
Bacon's *Advancement of Learning*
published.
The Gunpowder Plot.

Fletcher's *WOMAN'S PRIZE.**
Beaumont comes into an inherit-
ance upon death of elder brother,
Sir Henry.

1606
Shakespeare's *MACBETH.**
Jonson's *VOLPONE.**
Tourneur's *REVENGER'S TRAG-
EDY.**

The Red Bull theater built.

1607

Shakespeare's *ANTONY AND CLEOPATRA.**
Settlement of Jamestown, Virginia.

Beaumont's *KNIGHT OF THE BURNING PESTLE.**
Jonson's *VOLPONE*, with commendatory verses by Fletcher and Beaumont, published.
Beaumont and Fletcher collaboration begins.*

1608

Shakespeare's *CORIOLANUS,** *TIMON OF ATHENS,** *PERICLES.**
Chapman's *CONSPIRACY AND TRAGEDY OF CHARLES, DUKE OF BYRON.**
Richard Burbage leases Blackfriars Theatre for King's Company.
John Milton born.

Fletcher's *FAITHFUL SHEPHERDESS.**

1609

Shakespeare's *CYMBELINE;** *Sonnets* published.
Dekker's *Gull's Hornbook* published.

Beaumont and Fletcher's *PHILASTER,** *COXCOMB.** They affiliate with the King's Men.*

1610

Jonson's *ALCHEMIST.*
Chapman's *REVENGE OF BUSSY D'AMBOIS.**

Beaumont and Fletcher's *CAPTAIN,** *MAID'S TRAGEDY.**

1611

Authorized (King James) Version of the Bible published.
Shakespeare's *WINTER'S TALE,** *TEMPEST.**
Tourneur's *ATHEIST'S TRAGEDY.**

Jonson's *CATILINE*, with commendatory verses by Fletcher and Beaumont, published.
Beaumont and Fletcher's *KING AND NO KING.*

1612

Webster's *WHITE DEVIL.**
Richard Crashaw born.

Beaumont's epistle to Elizabeth, Countess of Rutland. He writes commendatory verses to Jonson's *EPICOENE*, first printed in the Jonson Folio of 1616.*

Fletcher and Shakespeare's *CAR-DENIO* (?).*

Fletcher marries Joan Herring (?).

1613

The Globe theater burned.

Webster's *DUCHESS OF MALFI.*

Middleton's *CHASTE MAID IN CHEAPSIDE.*

Sir Thomas Overbury murdered.

Beaumont's *INNER TEMPLE MASQUE.*

Beaumont marries Ursula Isley; collaboration with Fletcher ends.*

Fletcher and Shakespeare's *TWO NOBLE KINSMEN, HENRY VIII.*

Fletcher, Field, and Massinger's *HONEST MAN'S FORTUNE.*

1614

The Globe theater rebuilt.

The Hope Theatre opens.

Jonson's *BARTHOLOMEW FAIR.*

Fletcher's *WIT WITHOUT MONEY** (later revised?).

1616

Publication of Folio edition of Jonson's *Works.*

Death of Shakespeare.

Fall of Sir Edward Coke.

THE SCORNFUL LADY published.

Fletcher's *MAD LOVER.**

Death of Beaumont, March 6.

1617

Pocahontas presented at court.

Fletcher's *CHANCES.**

1618

Outbreak of Thirty Years War.

Execution of Raleigh.

Abraham Cowley born.

Fletcher's *LOYAL SUBJECT.*

1619

Synod of Dort.

Death of Queen Anne.

Field and Massinger's *FATAL DOWRY.*

THE MAID'S TRAGEDY and *A KING AND NO KING* published.

Fletcher and Massinger's *SIR JOHN VAN OLDEN BARNA-VELT.*

Fletcher's *HUMOROUS LIEU-TENANT.**

1620

Pilgrim Fathers land at Plymouth.

PHILASTER published.

Fletcher and Massinger's *CUS-TOM OF THE COUNTRY,** *FALSE ONE.**

1621

Middleton's *WOMEN BEWARE WOMEN.**
Robert Burton's *Anatomy of Melancholy* published.
Andrew Marvell born.

Fletcher and Massinger's *DOUBLE MARRIAGE.**
Fletcher's *PILGRIM** and *WILD GOOSE CHASE.**
Beaumont, Fletcher, and Massinger's *THIERRY AND THEODORET* published.

1622

Middleton and Rowley's *CHANGELING.**
Henry Vaughan born.

Fletcher and Massinger's *PROPHETESS, SPANISH CURATE, SEA VOYAGE.*

1623

Publication of Shakespeare First Folio.

Fletcher and Massinger's *LITTLE FRENCH LAWYER.**
Fletcher and Rowley's *MAID IN THE MILL.*

1624

Middleton's *GAME AT CHESS.*

Fletcher's *RULE A WIFE AND HAVE A WIFE, WIFE FOR A MONTH.*

1625

Death of King James I; accession of Charles I.

Fletcher's *FAIR MAID OF THE INN* (with Massinger, Webster, and Ford).
Death of Fletcher.

1626

Death of Bacon.
Death of Tourneur.

1627

Death of Middleton.

1628

Petition of Right.
Ford's *LOVER'S MELANCHOLY.*
Buckingham assassinated.

1631

Shirley's *TRAITOR.*
Death of Donne.

1632

Death of Dekker.*

1633
Donne's *Poems* published.
Massinger's *CITY MADAM*.*
Death of George Herbert.

1634
Death of Chapman, Marston, Webster.*

THE TWO NOBLE KINSMEN published.

1635
Sir Thomas Browne's *Religio Medici*.

1637
Death of Jonson.

THE ELDER BROTHER published.

1639
First Bishops' War
Death of Carew*

MONSIEUR THOMAS, WIT WITHOUT MONEY, ROLLO DUKE OF NORMANDY published.

1640
Short Parliament.
Long Parliament impeaches Laud.
Death of Massinger, Burton.

THE NIGHT WALKER, THE CORONATION published.

1641
Irish rebel.
Death of Heywood.

1642
Charles I leaves London; Civil War breaks out.
Shirley's *COURT SECRET*.
All theaters closed by Act of Parliament.

1643
Parliament swears to the Solemn League and Covenant.

1645
Ordinance for New Model Army enacted.

1646
End of First Civil War.

1647
Army occupies London.
Charles I forms alliance with Scots.

Beaumont and Fletcher First Folio published.